Dorothy Wor

Dorothy Wordsworth, Writer

PAMELA WOOF

The Wordsworth Trust Grasmere

First published 1988 by
The Wordsworth Trust
Dove Cottage, Grasmere, Cumbria LA22 9SH

British Library Cataloguing in Publication Data

Woof, Pamela
 Dorothy Wordsworth, writer
 1. English literature. Wordsworth,
 Dorothy – Critical studies
 I. Title
 828'.709

 ISBN 0–951061–66–6

Typeset by Gloucester Typesetting Services
and printed in Great Britain by
Cheney & Sons Limited
Banbury, Oxon OX16 7RH

Preface

This is an introduction to Dorothy and her prose: her letters, her account of the Green family disaster, her Journal Tours of Scotland and the Continent, her first Alfoxden and her last Rydal Journals, and above all her Journal of the days in Grasmere, one of the most celebrated and loved private diaries. It is an essay expanded from a lecture given at the Wordsworth Summer Conference, Grasmere, 1985, and afterwards published in *The Wordsworth Circle* for Spring 1986.

It became Dorothy's habit in the small notebooks of the Grasmere and the late Rydal Journals to abbreviate the central names to initials and to prefer an ampersand (&) to the word 'and'. 'And' has been printed out fully in the quotations from the Alfoxden and Grasmere Journals. In the greater spaciousness of the more considered *Recollections* of both the Scottish and Continental Tours Dorothy more usually wrote 'and'.

Some of the books I have consulted are acknowledged in the notes. It remains to record my indebtedness to the biographies of Dorothy Wordsworth by Ernest de Selincourt (1933) and Robert Gittings and Jo Manton (1985), and to Susan Levin's recent work on Dorothy's verse, *Dorothy Wordsworth and Romanticism* (Rutgers, 1987).

Pamela Woof
University of Newcastle upon Tyne

Dorothy Wordsworth 1771–1855:
Life and Writings

Selected Chronological List

1771   D born (25 December), Cockermouth, third child of Ann (Cookson) and John W, attorney and law-agent to Sir James Lowther. William twenty months old.

1778   D's mother dies (8 March), aged thirty. Her mother's cousin Elizabeth Threlkeld takes D to her home in Halifax, Yorkshire, where D lives until May 1787. Friendship with Jane Pollard, a neighbouring wool-merchant's daughter.

1779   William sent to Hawkshead Grammar School.

1781   Aged nine, D attends Dr and Mrs Wilkinson's boarding-school at Hipperholme, two miles from Halifax.

1783   D's father dies at Cockermouth (30 December). D does not return for the funeral.

1784   D's guardians, Uncles Richard Wordsworth and Christopher Cookson, transfer her to the day-school in Halifax of Miss Martha and Miss Hannah Mellin. D attends with Jane Pollard, goes regularly with 'Aunt' Threlkeld to Northgate End Unitarian Chapel and has access to the Halifax Old Subscription Library.

1787   D required to leave Halifax (May) and live with her Cookson grandparents above their draper's shop in Penrith. Meets her brothers again in school holidays. Friendship with Mary and Margaret (Peggy) Hutchinson, also orphans. William goes to St John's College, Cambridge (October). Grandfather dies (December).

1788   D's uncle William Cookson marries Dorothy Cowper, daughter of the vicar of Penrith (October) and takes D, after making short visits to Newcastle and Cambridge, to live with them at Forncett Rectory, Norfolk.

1789   D, aged seventeen, has a Sunday school of nine girls.

1790   William Wilberforce, friend of Uncle William, allows D ten guineas a year to distribute for charity (January). D plans and has for a time a more extensive school. Helps with Uncle's new baby. Receives long letter from William describing walking tour through the Alps (September); six-week visit from William (December–January).

1792   D goes with Uncle William Cookson, the new Canon of Windsor, and his family for three months' residence at Windsor (August–November).

1793   D *'fagging* . . . tolerably hard' at French, probably to correspond with Annette Vallon, by whom William has had a child in France but to whom he cannot return because of war. He is not invited to visit again at Forncett. D plans to go to Halifax (July).

1794   D arrives in Halifax (February) to visit 'Aunt' Elizabeth (now Mrs William Rawson) and to see William – after three years' absence – a visit of six weeks. With William to Windy Brow, Keswick, a farmhouse belonging to Raisley and William Calvert, schoolfriends of William (April–May). D makes visits to Uncle Richard Wordsworth near Whitehaven; a cousin, Mrs Barker, at Rampside, Furness; friends, the Miss Speddings, Armathwaite; Uncle Christopher Crackanthorpe (Cookson) at Newbiggin Hall, near Appleby; cousins, the Griffiths at Newcastle (until April 1795). D receives particular mention in a codicil to Raisley Calvert's will: some part of the £900 left to William for annuities is to be 'for the use and benefit' of D (October).

1795   D visits the Hutchinson sisters, now at their brother Tom's farm at Sockburn near Darlington (April). D with 'Aunt' Elizabeth at Halifax (May–September); attends Jane Pollard's wedding to John Marshall, linen-manufacturer of Leeds (August). Travels south and meets William in Bristol (22 September) and they go to Racedown Lodge, a house lent to William by the Pinney brothers, where they stay until July 1797, looking after the young Basil Montagu, not yet three when he first comes in September 1795.

1796   Peggy Hutchinson dies in the spring and Mary Hutchinson comes to Racedown for a long visit (November–June 1797).

1797   D meets Coleridge and describes him in a letter to Mary Hutchinson, who has just left (June). D meets Charles Lamb (July) and moves with William to Alfoxden House, Somerset, near Coleridge's cottage at Nether Stowey. Lives there until June 1798.

1798   D keeps a Journal at Alfoxden (20 January–22 May). D walks through the Wye Valley with William and is the subject of his impassioned tribute in *Tintern Abbey* (July).

Lyrical Ballads published (September/October). D travels with William and Coleridge to Hamburg and they stay there during September; D keeps a Journal. She leaves with William for Goslar (October) where they stay till February 1799.

1799 Return to England (April). D and William go to the Hutchinsons' farm at Sockburn where D stays until December. On 20 December she moves into a cottage at Town End, Grasmere (Dove Cottage), with William.

1800 D's younger sailor brother John arrives (January) and helps with the house and garden. D begins Grasmere Journal (14 May). Coleridge and his family visit and then move into Greta Hall, Keswick (July).

1802 With William, D goes to Calais during the Peace of Amiens and visits Annette and William's daughter Caroline aged nine (August). They stay with Basil Montagu (September) and D gets to know Mary as well as Charles Lamb. Goes to Gallow Hill near Brompton, Yorkshire, for the marriage of William to Mary Hutchinson (4 October), though is not present at the ceremony. Returns to Grasmere.

1803 The last entry in the Grasmere Journal (16 January). John, William and Mary's first child, born (18 June). D is a devoted aunt to the five children born between 1803 and 1810. With William and Coleridge, D leaves for six weeks Scottish Tour (mid-August), Coleridge taking his own route during September. D sees Burns' cottage, goes into the Highlands and meets Walter Scott. Begins to write up *Recollections* of the Tour for friends (not completed till May 1805).

1804 Helps to write out a copy of William's poems for Coleridge to take to Malta (April). Short tour with William into the Duddon Valley (September–October).

1805 Death off Weymouth Bay of her younger brother John, Captain of the East India ship the *Earl of Abergavenny* (5 February). 'Aunt' Rawson visits D (July); elder brother Richard buys D a pony for her health. With William a week's excursion by pony in the countryside about Ullswater (November). D writes a short Journal (this is later extensively revised by William and forms part of his Information for the Tourist in the *Guide to the Lakes*, 1822). D composes three stanzas, 'To My Niece Dorothy, a sleepless Baby'; these were published by

William in his *Poems* (1815) as 'The Cottager to her Infant. By a Female Friend'. Probably this year D writes the verses, 'Grasmere – a Fragment', where she describes herself as now 'an Inmate of this vale' – unpublished in D's lifetime. Molly Fisher, their old servant, and her brother John are guests on Christmas Day, D's birthday. Grasmere fiddler for dancing in Dove Cottage.

1806   D copies out and adds to the *Recollections* of the Scottish Tour (January–February). Coleridge returns from Malta (August); D describes the sad differences in him when the Wordsworths first see him (October) as they are on their way to Hall Farm, Coleorton, Leicestershire, a house lent by Sir George Beaumont, and big enough for the Wordsworths, three children, Sara Hutchinson and Coleridge, who joins them (December). D's poem, 'An address to a child in a high wind'; included as by a 'Female Friend of the Author' in William's *Poems* (1815).

1807   D is alone with the children, John, Dora, Thomas, at Coleorton (April–May) and writes a poem, 'The Mother's Return', the third and final poem of D's to be included in William's *Poems* (1815). There is no more verse until 1826. D and the Wordsworths return to Dove Cottage, Grasmere (June). The young Thomas de Quincey calls (November) and much later records his first impressions of D.

1808   D plays a large part in organising help for the Green children whose parents die in a snow-storm (March); her narrative account of the tragedy (not published till 1936) is influential in raising financial contributions. Moves with the Wordsworths to a large new house overlooking the valley, Allan Bank (May), big enough for the growing family and Coleridge (and two sons at weekends). Molly Fisher, their old servant, dies (June). De Quincey stays (November–February 1809).

1809   Helps refurnish Dove Cottage for De Quincey who moves in (October).

1810   Coleridge leaves Allan Bank for Keswick (May) and D is away when he stays again (October) on his way to London. Quarrel between Coleridge and William means that D does not see Coleridge for ten years. D makes visits: to the Beaumonts, with William, at their new Coleorton Hall (July); to Catherine Clarkson at Bury St Edmunds – passing through Cambridge (August–

September); to Charles and Mary Lamb in London, with Crabb Robinson to show her the sights; to Uncle William Cookson and his family, whom she has not seen since 1794. Back at Grasmere (23 October); to Elleray on Windermere, John Wilson's house, so that the children might escape scarlet fever. Composing 'a description or two for the finishing' of William's text to accompany Joseph Wilkinson's *Select Views* – later the *Guide to the Lakes* (November).

1811 Move to the Rectory, Grasmere (May). A new curate in Grasmere, William Johnson, 'so much in earnest'; the Wordsworths 'become regular church-goers . . . for the sake of the children' and D begins to turn to orthodox Christianity.

1812 Sudden death of Catharine, William and Mary's fourth child, aged almost four (4 June). D visits 'Aunt' Rawson, staying with Jane Marshall at Watermillock (July). Death of Thomas, the third child, aged six, from measles (1 December), D not at home (with the Marshalls again at Watermillock). Both children buried in the churchyard opposite the Rectory.

1813 William obtains Civil Service appointment as Distributor of Stamps for Westmorland: family income assured (April). The Wordsworths move to Rydal Mount, two miles away in the next valley (May). D, William and Mary live here for the rest of their lives.

1814 D stays with Miss Barker in Keswick, helping to nurse young Basil Montagu (January–April). *The Excursion* published (August). D goes with Sara Hutchinson to stay with Sara's brother Tom at his farm at Hindwell, Radnorshire (September–November). D invited by Annette and Caroline to attend Caroline's marriage in Paris to Jean Baptiste Baudouin (October). Marriage postponed in the hope that D can attend.

1815 France difficult to visit: Napoleon, escaped from Elba, enters Paris (March). Battle of Waterloo (June).

1816 Marriage of William's daughter Caroline (28 February), neither D nor William present; William allows Caroline £30 a year. Caroline's daughter born and named Louise Dorothée (December). D visits 'Aunt' Rawson in Halifax (October–February 1817).

1817 De Quincey marries Margaret Simpson, a local country girl (February): D's opinion, 'he is ruined'.

11

1818   D and William give much energy to the Lowther Tory cause in the elections; they are out, William 'canvassing' and perhaps D also, when Keats calls (June) and sticks a note 'over what I knew must be Miss Wordsworth's portrait'. D organises a six-week visit to Rydal of William Wilberforce and his family and household (August–October). D climbs Scafell Pike with Miss Barker (and a guide) and writes an account of the excursion to her friend, the former Grasmere curate William Johnson (October); she makes a second version of this and, revised by William and introduced as an 'extract from a letter to a Friend', it is published in the *Guide to the Lakes*, 1822. D's authorship is not revealed.

1820   D stays with her brother Christopher (a widower since 1815) at his rectory at Lambeth, London (April–July); visits to the dentist (50 guineas, but 'a delightful operator') for false teeth; visits to Willie, D's youngest nephew at Charterhouse School; visits to Charles and Mary Lamb and many other friends. With William and Mary D attends the wedding of Mary's cousin, Thomas Monkhouse, in London (8 July) and the whole party leaves for a tour on the Continent (July–November). Crabb Robinson joins them at Lucerne. They travel, walking for long stretches, through France, Belgium, Germany, Switzerland, by the St Gothard Pass to the Italian lakes and back over the Simplon Pass to Paris. D sees many of the scenes William saw in 1790. The Wordsworths spend September in Paris and see much of Annette and Caroline and her family (she has now two daughters, Dorothée and Anne); D writes a Journal of the Tour but does not include a description of the time in Paris. Coming back they stay with Miss Barker, now in a house at Boulogne, and are nearly shipwrecked in their first attempt to cross the Channel. They reach London (7 November), visit Christopher in Cambridge (now Master of Trinity) for a week (23 November), and D goes on to Playford Hall near Ipswich to stay with the Clarksons (December–January).

1821   D works at the Journal of the Tour of the Continent: 'to please him [William] I have amplified and arranged' (April–August). D recopies the Journal (October). It is intended for friends and for the children. Edward Quillinan, a lieutenant in the Dragoons and an admirer of William's poetry, and his wife stay at the Stepping

Stones at Rydal. D and Mary help nurse Mrs Quillinan after the birth of the Quillinans' second child, Rotha.

1822 The Quillinans move to Ivy Cottage, near Rydal Mount. Mrs Quillinan suffers bad accidental burning and D – the rest of the family being away – nurses her, attends her death-bed and arranges the funeral and finances (May–June). D takes a seven-week Tour in Scotland with Joanna Hutchinson (September–October). D does not revise and amplify her short Journal of this Tour, but revises instead the *Recollections* of the Scottish Tour of 1803, on Samuel Rogers suggesting publication; D hopes, for a short while, to make money for a further 'ramble'. This proposal comes to nothing and the *Recollections* are not published until 1874 (in the less revised version of 1806).

1824 D makes visits (March–June): Oxford (John now an undergraduate), London (at Thomas Monkhouse's), Cambridge (at Trinity College), Playford Hall (the Clarksons). D begins again to make some record of daily events (December); this continues as a sparse Journal with gaps until 1833.

1826 D stays mainly with Joanna Hutchinson and her brother Tom and his family (four children) now at Brinsop Court near Hereford (February–September), making various short visits: to the Hutchinsons' small farm nearby at Gwerndovennant (where D composes two poems); Manchester and Leamington (to see the young Jane Jewsbury, a new friend); a tour down the Wye Valley; Worcester (to stay with Miss Willes, a cousin of Lady Beaumont). D spends October with the Beaumonts at Coleorton.

1827 D in Halifax with 'Aunt' Rawson (June–September).

1828 D takes a holiday with Joanna Hutchinson and her eldest 'sailor' brother Henry in the Isle of Man (June–July). D keeps house for her nephew John in his first curacy at Whitwick near Coleorton and helps in parish work and visiting (November–June 1829).

1829 D spends a month at Cambridge with Christopher (February). Becomes ill at Whitwick (April) and Mary Wordsworth comes to nurse her. D returns via Halifax, staying with 'Aunt' Rawson, now 83 and a widow (late June–September). Back at Rydal D has periods of great pain but goes out in the 'Family phaeton', or is pulled in a small carriage/bath chair along the new terrace in the garden by James Dixon, the Wordsworths' gardener and handyman.

1830 D regains strength. Makes arrangements for Hartley Coleridge to be housed and looked after in Grasmere. William extends the top terrace in the garden. D makes two short stays in Ambleside with her Whitehaven cousin's daughter, Dorothy Wordsworth, now Mrs Benson Harrison. Her nephew John, now settled in a living at Moresby, Cumberland, marries Isabella Curwen of Workington Hall and Belle Isle (11 October); D does not attend, but describes the wedding from her niece Dora's report.

1831 D stays for a few days with the Curwens on Belle Isle (September). Severely ill again (December), and diary entries cease until October 1832.

1832 D composes 'Loving and Liking. Irregular Verses Addressed to a Child'; it was published in William's *Poems* (1836) as by a 'Female Friend of the Author'. Another late poem, 'The Floating Island at Hawkshead', appeared in William's collection of 1842 and now the female friend is identified as 'D.W.'. This was the fifth and last of D's poems to be published in her lifetime. D has to take laudanum regularly.

1833 D has another relapse, but rallies. A self-educated Cockermouth artist, Samuel Crosthwaite, comes to paint William and paints D too (September).

1834 Death of Coleridge (July) and of Charles Lamb (December). D 'well and ill'.

1835 William's daughter Dora ill. D receives a letter from Annette begging her to intercede with William to provide enough for Caroline so that she might still have £30 a year (the £400 lump sum with which William replaced the annuity is insufficient to keep the terms of the marriage contract) (April). But D is already in decline. Sara Hutchinson dies (June). D's opium dose is reduced.

1835–1855 D, suffering probably from what is now known as pre-senile dementia, has long periods of mental derangement; there are a few short letters and verses in lucid intervals. She is cared for lovingly by William and Mary and the household at Rydal Mount.

1841 Dora marries Edward Quillinan at Bath (May).

1847 Death of Dora (July).

1850 Death of William (April).

1855 Death of D (January): 'our dear Sister', wrote Mary Wordsworth to her brother Thomas's widow, Mary, 'was released after her gradual but *fitful* sinking and some few hours of peaceful and anxious waiting.'

1859 Death of Mary Wordsworth (January).

Dorothy Wordsworth, Writer

The night very stormy – My Flower-pots blown down – I was very ill after dinner – Why or wherefore I know not – pain – sickness – head-ache perspiration – heat & Cold – but, being exhausted & free from pain I slept pretty well though often up & awaked This morning bright but cold, & a hail-shower falls from dazzling silver – & dark clouds to remind us of past times & warn us not to expect a calm suddenly – Reading Quarles Have finished Mr Edgeworths Life & am reading Saturdays Mag – & Sir Chris^r Wren's Life[1] – The Evening very stormy – Rain by pailfuls driven against my windows [*RJ*, Wednesday 19 February[2]]

Loveliest of Sabbath morns – How I long to be free of the open air! The Birds are all singing – Rooks very busy The earth & air & all that I behold seems a preparation for worship and sabbath rest – Bird & Beast have this one day's security, from snare or slaughter read Horsley & Bible & a few Essays – All at Church except William. [*RJ*, Sunday 6 April]

Two Journal entries of 1834. Dorothy is over sixty and ill, and her writing now is quite private. It was always fairly private: one or two readers for the earlier letters and journals, and even for the most public of her works only a limited readership in manuscript. She wrote up a careful journal account, for example, of the walking tour in Scotland that she made with Wordsworth in 1803; and in 1808, in order to raise money for children who were suddenly made orphans she told the story of the parents, George and Sarah Green of Grasmere, and their deaths one March Saturday in snow and mist on hills close to home. A friend, Catherine Clarkson – 'She is the wife of Mr Clarkson who was the grand mover of the main efforts for the abolition of the Slave Trade' was the way Dorothy introduced her in August 1805 – suggested publication. Dorothy's refusal was firm: 'much as I should detest the idea of setting myself up as an Author' (9 December 1810),[3] she replied, making her own wishes in the matter very clear, she felt strongly that from the children's point of view even anonymous publication would be harmful. Yet, despite her inclinations for privacy, it has been her posthumous fate to have many readers.

These brief late entries of 1834, their phrases hurried onto the page, impress us at once as Dorothy Wordsworth's; they have, in little, characteristics that have been hers through the years of practice in writing. There is the ability to begin at once with the facts, omitting all introduction, 'The night very stormy'. There are the varieties of prose rhythms which here range from the staccato 'My Flower-pots blown down' and 'Rooks very busy' to the longer flow of words that echo a line from *Tintern Abbey*, written nearly forty years before: 'The earth & air & all that I behold seems', then, oddly, not 'full of blessings', but 'a preparation for worship and sabbath rest'. There is the expression of feeling, here, the plain yearning in the sudden exclamation of a line that is almost blank verse: 'Loveliest of Sabbath morns – How I long to be free of the open air!'. There is the swift movement away from such a mood to the outside world: 'The Birds are all singing'. There is the consciousness of her brother – his is the one name mentioned (not at Church). There is the moralising – 'prosing' as Dorothy herself called it: the 'dark clouds' that 'warn us not to expect a calm suddenly'. There is the sense of vigorous activity of weather – pots blown down, rain driven. There is the careful recording of illness. There are the contrasts – 'dazzling silver – & dark'. There is the move towards memory: the 'dark clouds to remind us of past times'. There are the books read and named, but with no comment, and these, now, in 1834, are essays, sermons, the Bible and biographies – rarely fiction and poetry. There is the domestic word – 'Rain by pailfuls' – and the inability to find meaning – 'Why or wherefore I know not'. There is the general sense of someone alive to circumstance but at the mercy of it, and, like 'Bird & Beast', grateful for 'this one day's security', and never unaware that the night is stormy.

From the Grasmere to the late Rydal journals, by such notes as these we recognise Dorothy, and know why so many readers, some indeed who rarely turn to Wordsworth's poetry, find the Journals so fresh, so readable, so re-readable at any entry, anywhere. Poetry makes a stand against Time; but we read the Journals and enter the time and seasons of Dorothy Wordsworth in a particular place, and we are carried, as she was, and as we, too, often are, somewhat helplessly, on time's quick ups and downs.

Dorothy was not a primitive; she learned to write. Like all writers she built on and used other writers. Wordsworth's verse was constantly invoked to give point to her thoughts, and before he had a body of work she resorted to that of others. Shylock's phrase for the Merchant Antonio's ships, 'squandered abroad', seemed to Dorothy apt to describe the scattered Wordsworth orphans, and twice, in January 1788 and 1790, she used it in letters to Jane Pollard, her friend from girlhood days in Halifax, 'How we are squandered abroad'. As late as July 1793 she referred Jane to James Beattie's *Minstrel* (1771) so that Jane could get an idea of William's character, which, in Dorothy's view, was not unlike that of Beattie's hero, Edwin. She quotes only some two lines from the following two verses of the poem and assumes that Jane will fill in the rest:

> *In truth he was a strange and wayward wight,*
> *Fond of each gentle,* and each dreadful scene.
> In darkness, and in storm, he found delight:
> Nor less, than when on ocean-wave serene
> The southern sun diffused his dazzling shene.
> Even sad vicissitude amused his soul:
> And if a sigh would sometimes intervene,
> And down his cheek a tear of pity roll,
> A sigh, a tear, so sweet, he wish'd not to control.
>
> (Stanza 22)

19

> *And oft he traced the uplands*, to survey,
> When o'er the sky advanced the kindling dawn,
> The crimson cloud, blue main, and mountain grey,
> And lake, dim-gleaming on the smoky lawn:
> Far to the west the long long vale withdrawn,
> Where twilight loves to linger for a while;
> And now he faintly kens the bounding fawn,
> And villager abroad at early toil.
> But, lo! the sun appears! and heaven, earth, ocean,
>   smile.

(Stanza 20)

Indeed, she expects Jane to know 'the whole character of Edwin', a shepherd-boy of exquisite sensibility who had skill on the lyre 'to modulate the artful strain'. Beattie's sub-title to *The Minstrel* is, not surprisingly, *The Progress of Genius*. Such literary help in describing William was useful, for Jane, living in Halifax, had not met Dorothy's brothers; indeed, for many years, after Dorothy had left the Halifax home of her mother's cousin when she was fifteen, Jane did not see Dorothy either, and Dorothy settled into a style of letter-writing that could not presume on recent conversation. One of her friendships in fact grew entirely out of letters, that with Lady Beaumont. The letters began after Sir George Beaumont, whom the Wordsworths did not then know, in 1803, in admiration for Wordsworth as a poet and in hopes to make it easier for him and Coleridge to talk and write again with their former closeness, had given Wordsworth a small property at Keswick, not far from Coleridge's house, Greta Hall. Through the vivid letters friendship came, and when Dorothy met Lady Beaumont, finally, in November 1806, she and Sir George were the 'delightful good people' Dorothy already knew and loved.

She could write to friends for years without seeing them, simply providing news. 'I have only talked about ourselves and about ordinary things', she tells Catherine Clarkson in October 1804. These ordinary things are what we value: the way William 'takes out the umbrella and I daresay, stands stock-still under it during many a rainy half-hour, in the middle of road or field' (13 February 1804); the way Dorothy in 1810 saw the gateway of St John's, the Cambridge college where Wordsworth had been a student twenty years before, 'the light from a distance streaming along the level pavement – Thy Freshman's days came into my mind and I could have burst into tears', but she did not weep; she 'supped upon a Lamb chop', and next morning, as she contemplated the great statue of Newton whose 'Prism and silent face' had so affected Wordsworth, she had feelings that 'were I am sure sublime – though dear Mr Clarkson did now and then disturb me by pointing out the wrinkles in the silk stockings, the buckles etc.' (14 August 1810); the way her niece Dora, aged ten, gave them 'one terrible struggle' at being washed all over in cold water every day when the Ambleside doctor Mr Scambler suggested that this was just as good as bathing in sea water (15 August 1815); the way Dorothy was vexed when Dora, as a young woman of twenty-three, submitted to a French hairdresser – 'I cannot condone the notion of seeing her decked (nay not decked – depressed) by big curls – and Bows and Giraffe Wires' (21 May 1828). Dorothy perhaps forgot that forty years earlier the vivid everyday picture that she had given Jane Pollard was of herself as a fifteen-year old, sleepy and with her 'Hair to curl' in her grandmother's house in Penrith, 'sitting in my bed-gown, my hair out of curl and hanging about my face, with a small candle beside me' (6 August 1787). The letters are full of such vignettes. At the beginning there is the scene of Dorothy and her grandmother with an old shirt to mend and so 'my Grandmr and I have to set our heads together and contrive the most notable way of doing it' (November 1787); and towards the end there is the different contriving to find money for lodgings, hats, shoes and coats for 'poor Hartley', Coleridge's once brilliant and enchanting child, now a man of thirty-four 'calling at this house or that . . . housing at night in Barns' (5 March 1830).

In the very early letter-writing years Dorothy had the time to send accounts as full as any we might expect from the heroine of an eighteenth-century epistolary novel; indeed, a novel of that kind, Richardson's *Clarissa*, which she found so 'interesting when I first read [it] at 14 years of age' (30 August 1807), must have been a model. 'You shall have a full Description', she told Jane Pollard, 'of my Manner of Life and of the Impression things make upon me' (8 May 1792). And so, in the summer of that year, 1792, when Dorothy, aged twenty, went for three months to Windsor with the young family of her Uncle William Cookson, the new Canon, Jane duly received from Dorothy's pen a full description of Windsor Castle and its Prospects, of George III walking on the terrace and talking with the little Cookson children, of the Queen in her phaeton, and of Dorothy's own 'most severe tremblings and palpitations during the first Dance' (16 October 1792). In February 1793, offering Jane yet another, earlier, analysis of the unknown William, she showed that she, like her contemporary, Jane Austen, could marshal the vocabulary of psychological abstractions: she remarked William's 'Virtues', 'violence of Affection', 'sort of restless watchfulness', 'Tenderness that never sleeps' and 'Delicacy of Manners'. She then moved to the concrete, and, with a prophetic nostalgia, entered into her own vision of happiness:

When I think of Winter I hasten to furnish our little Parlour, I close the Shutters, set out the Tea-table, brighten the Fire. When our Refreshment is ended I produce our Work, and William brings his book to our Table and contributes at once to our Instruction and amusement, and at Intervals we lay aside the Book and each hazard our observations upon what has been read without the fear of Ridicule or Censure. We talk over past days, we do not sigh for any Pleasures beyond our humble Habitation

'The central point of all our joys'. Oh Jane! [16 February 1793]

Jane would have easily recognised Cowper's 'Winter Evening' ('Now stir the fire, and close the shutters fast', *The Task* iv, 36), particularly as Dorothy included the 'Tea-table', Cowper's 'cups that cheer but not inebriate'. But she would have had to look into the very newly-published *Descriptive Sketches* by 'W. Wordsworth' for the winter hut to which the Swiss mountain man returns at evening,

> The hut which from the hills his eyes employs
> So oft, the central point of all his joys.
> (*Descriptive Sketches* (1793), 570–1)

Dorothy's characteristic addition to the Romantic hut image is that in the 'humble Habitation' they would 'talk over past days' – as indeed they come to do; one thinks of Dorothy telling William nearly ten years later at Dove Cottage of how she used as a child to chase butterflies 'a little but that I was afraid of brushing the dust off their wings, and did not catch them' (*DWJ*, 14 March 1802).[4] But here, in 1793, she was only twenty-one when she envisaged the joy of talking 'Of summer days when we were young', to use Wordsworth's words from one of the poems he wrote in 1802 about those butterflies of childhood. In that same letter to Jane of February 1793, she turned to the poetry of Goldsmith to define her grief at the separation from her brothers: '. . . we have been compelled to spend our youth far asunder. "We drag at each remove a lengthening Chain" ', she told Jane, who no doubt could supply the preceding lines from Goldsmith's *Traveller*:

> Where'er I roam, whatever realms to see,
> My heart untravelled fondly turns to thee;
> Still to my brother turns with ceaseless pain,
> And drags at each remove a lengthening chain.
> (*The Traveller*, 7–10)

The following year, 1794, Jane was presumed to be familiar with the language of the picturesque. Dorothy described to her the prospect from a farm-house near Keswick where she was living for a few weeks with her brother. She had taken an independent step, left her Uncle William Cookson's rectory and assured everyone, even Jane, of the 'cheapness of living' in Keswick; she told her critical Aunt Crackanthorpe, her other Cookson uncle's wife, that her 'supper and breakfast [were] of bread and milk and my dinner chiefly of potatoes, from choice' (21 April 1794). There was feast enough for the eyes: 'we command', she wrote at the same time to Jane, 'a view of the whole vale of Keswick (the vale of Elysium, as Mr Grey calls it)'. The poet Thomas Gray had thus characterised the valley in 1769 when he came to the Lake District and wrote a journal of his tour. This was published in 1775 and had been reprinted several times since. Jane would have understood the reference, and would no doubt have responded also to the same fashionably picturesque language of Dorothy's further remarks, 'on one side Skiddaw towers sublime and . . . the middle part of the vale is of beautiful cultivated grounds interspersed with cottages'. The Sublime and the Beautiful had been aesthetic categories since Edmund Burke's *Essay* of 1756. Another of Dorothy's teachers in observation was the Cumbrian-born William Gilpin, who published his famous *Observations relative . . . to Picturesque Beauty* in 1786; this was based on his own long experience of the Lakes and on a particular tour of 1772. Among much else, he drew attention to the different appearances of shadows and reflections, and he took delight in 'grand echoes' and 'distant repetitions'. Dorothy likewise noted these transitory effects. Here, in a Grasmere entry, she catches at the one time both reflection and echo:

The lake was now most still and reflected the beautiful yellow and blue and purple and grey colours of the sky. We heard a strange sound in the Bainriggs wood as we were floating on the water it *seemed* in the wood but it must have been above it, for presently we saw a raven very high above us – it called out and the Dome of the sky seemed to echo the sound – it called again and again as it flew onwards, and the mountains gave back the sound, seeming as if from their center a musical bell-like answering to the birds hoarse voice. We heard both the call of the bird and the echo after we could see him no longer. [*DWJ*, 26 July 1800]

In her early sensibility Dorothy is entirely at one with her age and time. Neither Jane Austen's earnest heroine of feeling, Fanny Price in *Mansfield Park*, nor even that character of impetuous and excessive heart, Marianne Dashwood in *Sense and Sensibility*, could have gone further than Dorothy in the Romantic response to nature: 'The melancholy Pleasure', she told Jane Pollard in August 1793, 'of walking in a Grove or Wood while the yellow leaves are showering around me, is grateful to my mind beyond even the exhilarating charms of the budding trees, while Music echoes through the Grove.'

Her critical terminology is equally correct. She discusses Wordsworth's first published poems in ways that Dr Johnson would have approved; she notes beauties and faults:

. . . by moveless when applied to the Swan he [Wordsworth] means that sort of motion which is smooth without agitation; it is a very beautiful epithet but ought to have been cautiously used, he ought at any rate only to have hazarded it once, instead of which it occurs three or four times. [16 February 1793]

The word 'viewless' similarly becomes a blemish when used 'more than once or twice'. When Dorothy is closer to the actual writing of the poetry, there is little recorded criticism of it, though clearly her judgment remains important. Of a stanza in 'Farewell, thou little nook of mountain ground', Wordsworth said in 1802, 'I find neither D[orothy]. nor C[oleridge]. understand it. . . . I have been obliged to alter the [last] stanza'

(14 June 1802). Despite this instance, it would seem that Dorothy progressively absorbed rather than challenged Wordsworth's critical stance. When Sara Hutchinson had the temerity to offer criticism of 'The Leech-gatherer' she received not only a fine defence from Wordsworth but a firm rebuke from Dorothy:

When you happen to be displeased with what you suppose to be the tendency or moral of any poem which William writes, ask yourself whether you have hit upon the real tendency and true moral, and above all never think that he writes for no reason but merely because a thing happened – and when you feel any poem of his to be tedious, ask yourself in what spirit it was written – whether merely to tell the tale and be through with it, or to illustrate a particular character or truth etc. etc.

I am glad that you have found out how to bake bread in my way . . . [14 June 1802]

The partisanship is for bread as well as poetry, and bread generally takes over as the subject-matter of the regular letters to Jane Pollard (now Jane Marshall). No longer is there the shared pleasure of 1787 in a 'comical poem' addressed to a louse and a 'very pretty' one to a mountain daisy;[5] Jane, during the Wordsworths' later years at Dove Cottage, and afterwards at Rydal Mount, is offered Dorothy's fears about whooping cough for the children and her anxieties about the hiring of servants. But when there is, exceptionally, a literary judgment, we see that there is no falling-off in Dorothy's perceptions. Here is her astute criticism in 1815 of Walter Scott's first (anonymous) novel:

With respect to Waverley the author has completely failed in one point – you care not a farthing for the hero, Waverley, and as you observe the Scotch Characters are so outrageously masked by peculiarities that there is no pleasure in contemplating them – indeed in the delineation of character he greatly fails throughout – and as usual the love is sickening. The highland manners and costume are the most interesting feature in the work. [18 February 1815]

Even in the early days, before Wordsworth's children came, and Dorothy read, *inter alia*, so much Shakespeare, Milton, Spenser and Chaucer, there is no such extended comment as that on *Waverley*. A reaction is rare, and there is almost no analysis:

After tea I read aloud the 11th Book of Paradise Lost. We were much impressed and also melted into tears. [*DWJ*, 2 February 1802]

Why? Was it Eve's lament that she had to leave 'these happy Walks and Shades', or Adam's despair at the vision of wars to come and the 'peace that corrupts no less', or the Paradise Garden itself become 'The haunt of Seals and Orcs and Sea-mews clang'? The tears are not analysed. For the youthful De Quincey, by contrast, a diary is a means of investigation. He uses it to probe the complications of literature: he discusses at length, say, the character of Telemachus in the *Odyssey*; or tries out words and ideas, and when he makes a fine statement he is so pleased he writes it down:

I just said – 'My imagination flies, like Noah's dove, from the ark of my mind . . . and finds no place on which to rest the sole of her foot except Coleridge, Wordsworth and Southey' [*A Diary of Thomas de Quincey 1803*, ed. Horace A. Eaton, 1928, p. 209]

He is getting to know himself. To some extent this must have been a by-product of Dorothy's Journals but it was not their aim. She does not ponder on why it was *The Winter's Tale* that she chose to read on that July day in 1802 just before she and Wordsworth left Grasmere to go into Yorkshire to see Mary Hutchinson and so establish the approaching October marriage. Was it the play's farewell to the pastoral world or some undiscerned empathy for the jealousy one person can feel within a close group of three?

Dorothy was familiar with the blank verse of poets from Shakespeare to Coleridge, and that her early prose

27

could fall into the iambic line is not surprising. Here, in what was probably her first Journal, written while she and Wordsworth – in order to be near Coleridge – were living at Alfoxden, Somerset, in 1798, we can feel Wordsworth's influence:

William went with me to the wood. Coleridge very ill. It was a mild, pleasant afternoon, but the evening became very foggy; when I was near Woodlands, the fog overhead became thin, and I saw the shapes of the Central Stars. Again it closed, and the whole sky was the same. [*DWJ*, 6 March 1798]

A wood, illness, fog; then, a sudden clearing, and in a perfect line, a glimpse of the significant heavens,

and I saw the shapes of the Central Stars.

It is like the illumination of that earlier night-sky that Dorothy had described in January:

Went to Poole's [Coleridge's good friend and neighbour, Thomas Poole, a prosperous tanner at Nether Stowey] after tea. The sky spread over with one continuous cloud, whitened by the light of the moon, which, though her dim shape was seen, did not throw forth so strong a light as to chequer the earth with shadows. At once the clouds seemed to cleave asunder, and left her in the centre of a black-blue vault. She sailed along, followed by multitudes of stars, small, and bright, and sharp. Their brightness seemed concentrated, (half-moon). [*DWJ*, 25 January 1798]

This, Dorothy's first night-piece, is totally impersonal: there is no viewer. When Wordsworth used it almost straightaway in his poem 'A Night-piece', he gave it drama by having the sky's appearance witnessed, not simply described in isolation; in the poem a 'pensive traveller', his 'unobserving eye / Bent earthwards' is startled by 'The clear Moon, and the glory of the heavens'. And only at this point does Wordsworth move into description which is close to Dorothy's, 'There, in a black-blue vault she sails along . . .' It was perhaps that adding of the personal that encouraged Dorothy in her later March entry of sky-change to declare that it was indeed she who had had that momentary glimpse,

and I saw the shapes of the Central Stars.

It is not that night walking was new to her in 1798 – she had written to Jane Pollard in 1791, 'I am particularly fond of a moonlight or twilight walk – it is at this time that I think most of my absent friends' (23 May 1791). Then, when she was nineteen, moonlight was for feeling; now, in the Alfoxden Journal of 1798, she tries to describe it. The Alfoxden Journal is altogether more a sketch book for descriptive exercises than a diary. Dorothy seems deliberately to pursue changing appearances. Night scenes and moonscapes were a particular challenge, and there are a dozen or so of these in the Alfoxden Journal, a journal that covers only the late winter and early spring of 1798. Events are cursorily noted, even misremembered: while Wordsworth and Dorothy could indeed have gone 'to Poole's after tea' on 25 January, they could not, on three days before his return on 9 February, have 'walked with Coleridge'. Dorothy's first accuracy is for her own extended sea, land and night scapes. But the simple action creeps upon the Journal, and after three weeks, 'William gathered sticks'.[6] Several days of description further on, there is a mere mention of Basil – 'returned to Wm and Basil. A shower met us in the wood, and a ruffling breeze'. Basil was the young son of a fairly recent friend, Basil Montagu; his mother was dead and his father was busy in chambers in London. He was just five when with the Wordsworths at Alfoxden, and they had given him a loving country home since the end of 1795. His progress and his play do not feature in the Alfoxden Journal, and this again demonstrates that Dorothy's primary interest was the description of the natural scene. Well over a month into the Journal, there is a casual encounter:

Met a razor-grinder with a soldier's jacket on, a knapsack upon his back, and a boy to drag his wheel. [*DWJ*, 22 February 1798]

There is no attempt to get his story; Dorothy quickly returns to sea and wood and wind. But the activities have begun and she enters now into her own mixed style of diary-keeping: she hangs out the linen; fetches eggs from Coombe; keeps an eye on the progress of the spring; notes the hedgerows becoming green, and the stitchwort budding; and comments that Mary Wollstone-craft's *Life*[7] has come and that William has been engaged in wearisome composition.

The manuscript of the Journal is lost. All we have in writing are the first four sentences of the first entry, that for 20 January 1798. These are in Wordsworth's hand in a verse notebook. Yet they are clearly Dorothy's composition; and they gave Wordsworth an idea. They are:

The green paths down the hillsides are channels for streams. The young wheat is streaked by silver lines of water running between the ridges, the sheep are gathered together on the slopes. After the wet dark days, the country seems more populous. It peoples itself in the sunbeams. [*DWJ*, 20 January 1798]

These short, squat statements, firm and hard grammatically, are about vital movement: paths are streams, wheat is streaked by lines of water running and sheep are crowding. The 'wet dark days' are gone, the world is busy and Dorothy's tentative metaphor is right – 'the country seems more populous'. She turns the notion into a verb and makes it definite, 'It peoples itself in the sunbeams'. It is this metaphor, not the precise observation of hillsides and sheep, that seems to have attracted Wordsworth, and given him the idea for the paradox of a 'peopled solitude': he speaks of a lonely landscape as,

these populous slopes

With all their groves and with their murmurous woods,
Giving a curious feeling to the mind
Of peopled solitude.

(*Poetical Works*, v, 341)

Since each of Dorothy's entries is a separate entity and

unconnected with any other, a favourite word-for-the-moment can be obsessively used, so that it is the word 'streaked' that is evidence here, despite Wordsworth's hand-writing, of Dorothy's authorship of the first four Alfoxden sentences: the statement that the 'wheat is streaked' is followed within six days by 'The sea perfectly calm blue, streaked with deeper colour by the clouds'; 'The sea of a sober grey, streaked by the deeper grey clouds'; and 'the blue-grey sea, shaded with immense masses of cloud, not streaked'.

Dorothy tries for effect in these painterly exercises. Oaks, for instance, are 'like the columns of a ruin'; with ivy twisting round, they are 'like bristled serpents'; trees with their upper boughs stiff and erect are 'like black skeletons'; there are 'the tall and slender pillars of the unbranching oaks'; and soon we find that 'The crooked arm of the old oak tree points upwards to the moon'.[8] These Gothic touches are soon discarded. Similes in the later, Grasmere Journals have an observed and domestic aptness:

The moonshine like herrings in the water. [*DWJ*, 31 October 1800]

The snow blew from Helvellyn horizontally like smoke

and, as she does when she likes a phrase, Dorothy repeats this immediately,

the Spray of the unseen Waterfall like smoke [*DWJ*, 4 November 1800]

There are few extended similes, or elaborate metaphors; these would take Dorothy too far from the visible. The 'one busy highway' of daffodils, with 'here and there a little knot and a few stragglers a few yards higher up', is, for Dorothy, a developed piece of image-making. These small wild daffodils by Ullswater have already been endowed with life as dancing partners to the wind: they have 'tossed and reeled and danced and . . . laughed'

31

while some – and here Dorothy uses the brief domestic comparison that is her usual mode – have 'rested their heads upon [the mossy] stones as on a pillow for weariness' (*DWJ*, 15 April 1802). There is no forcing for effect here. In this instance, as elsewhere, Dorothy seems doubly alive to the wind, and her language flows to create the scene as surely as the trees or flowers bend to that element.

But it was in the company of Coleridge and Wordsworth at Alfoxden that Dorothy entered into her real education as a writer, and the Alfoxden Journal is her brilliant juvenilia. She sets about it with a will. When she records, 'Upon the whole an uninteresting evening', she does not mean that the conversation was dull, but that she found nothing in particular to observe. A landscape could be judged 'mildly interesting'. This is a usage she retains: walking in 'the black quarter' (the Easedale valley) in September 1800, she notes, 'The patches of corn very interesting'. The three of them, the two poets and Dorothy, despite the time of year, were constantly sitting, even lying down, in that Somerset winter and spring of 1798. There is something almost predatory in the deliberation: 'Again sat down to feed upon the prospect' (*DWJ*, 26 February 1798), or 'Cottage gardens the object of our walk' (*DWJ*, 7 February 1798). Later she and William will cultivate a cottage garden, but now, at Alfoxden, Dorothy is learning to look, and poems of Wordsworth and Coleridge informed and were informed by that looking. Dorothy begins to linger on both the detail and the prospect:

In the deep Coombe, as we stood upon the sunless hill, we saw miles of grass, light and glittering, and the insects passing. [*DWJ*, 8 February 1798]

The singing shape of this sentence, with the dying fall of its hanging participle at the end, is inseparable from the lift and fall of the content – the exhilaration of the eye in the movement from the deep Coombe upon the sunless hill to the miles of grass, light and glittering, and then its contraction to the detail of insects passing. The permanence of earth, the forces of darkness and light, and the transitoriness of the living, are suggested by this brief landscape. Wordsworth will remember part of the rhythm and will describe an early London morning as,

> All bright and glittering in the smokeless air.

Indeed, the sonnet from which that line comes, 'Composed upon Westminster Bridge', is closely and tantalisingly bound up with Dorothy's writing. Here is her description from her Journal for 1802:

> The houses were not overhung by their cloud of smoke and they were spread out endlessly, yet the sun shone so brightly with such a pure light that there was even something like the purity of one of nature's own grand spectacles. [*DWJ*, 31 July 1802]

She notes the smokelessness and suggests that London (in its dawn stillness) could have the qualities of permanence and moral grandeur that we associate with nature. 'Never', wrote Wordsworth, 'did sun more beautifully steep / In his first splendor valley, rock, or hill.' Wordsworth's account was probably written before Dorothy's: he wrote it (or was it only part of it?), he said long afterwards, 'on the roof of a coach, on my way to France, Sepbr. 1802'. It was in fact August when they went to France, and Dorothy's account was probably not written up until after Wordsworth's wedding and they were all back home again in Grasmere in October. We cannot absolutely know which is echo and which anticipation; their common source was probably a conversation on that July morning in London.

Coleridge, two years before Wordsworth echoed Dorothy's 'light and glittering', had found stimulus in Dorothy's Alfoxden writings – the small dull moon and the one red leaf of 'Christabel' are famous instances.

This alone must have encouraged her to observe and describe. On a winter's day in February, she and Wordsworth 'Walked to Woodlands, and to the waterfall' and Dorothy observed

adder's-tongue and the ferns green in the low damp dell. These plants now in perpetual motion from the current of the air; in summer only moved by the drippings of the rocks. [*DWJ*, 10 February 1798]

Coleridge's poem of the previous summer, *This Lime Tree Bower*, could have prompted Dorothy, in winter, to look at the ferns and to remember the detail of their summer movement as he had described it; his poem had pointed to the 'ferny rock' in the dell,

> Whose plumy ferns forever nod and drip
> Spray'd by the waterfall

In his later 1800 note to the plumy ferns – which have now become 'long lank weeds' – Coleridge in his turn added Dorothy's information: 'in some countries [these are] called adder's tongue'.

The eye that can apprehend differences in seasonal fern movement is akin to the ear that likes to distinguish sounds. Here, with one of her characteristic strong verbs, Dorothy animates the trees to roaring yet still remains aware of the rustling beneath:

The trees almost *roared*, and the ground seemed in motion with the multitudes of dancing leaves, which made a rustling sound, distinct from that of the trees. Still the asses pastured in quietness under the hollies ... The wind beat furiously ... [*DWJ*, 1 February 1798]

In Wordsworth's *Peter Bell*, just on Dorothy's heels, is that same roaring:

> The woods, my friends, are round you roaring,
> The woods are roaring like a sea
>
> (ll. 12-13)

while Dorothy's contrast – the furious wind, and the

asses pasturing in quietness under the hollies – is close to one of the central images of *Peter Bell* – the stillness of an ass in the midst of violence.

The interplay between Dorothy's journals and the poems of Wordsworth and Coleridge can be demonstrated richly and variously, and it must have invigorated all three writers. Coleridge's Conversation Poems could have taught Dorothy to look not only at details like the fern, but also at the larger view. In his 1796 *Reflections on Having Left a Place of Retirement*, Coleridge takes us from foreground to far-distance through a landscape that, like a painting by Claude, allows us to wander in it towards a far-off place:

> Oh! what a goodly scene! *Here* the bleak mount,
> The bare bleak mountain speckled thin with sheep;
> Grey clouds, that shadowing spot the sunny fields;
> And river, now with bushy rocks o'erbrow'd,
> Now winding bright and full, with naked banks;
> And seats, and lawns, the Abbey and the wood,
> And cots, and hamlets, and faint city-spire;
> The Channel *there*, the Islands and white sails,
> Dim coasts, and cloud-like hills and shoreless Ocean –
> It seem'd like Omnipresence!
>
> (ll. 29–38)

Dorothy produces her own extensive view; it is careful:

The Welsh hills capped by a huge range of tumultuous white clouds. The sea, spotted with white, of a bluish grey in general, and streaked with darker lines. The near shores clear; scattered farm houses, half-concealed by green mossy orchards, fresh straw lying at the doors; hay-stacks in the fields. Brown fallows, the springing wheat, like a shade of green over the brown earth, and the choice meadow plots, full of sheep and lambs, of a soft and vivid green; a few wreaths of blue smoke, spreading along the ground; the oaks and beeches in the hedges retaining their yellow leaves; the distant prospect on the land side, islanded with sunshine; the sea, like a basin full to the margin; the dark fresh-ploughed fields; the turnips of a lively rough green. Returned through the wood. [*DWJ*, 24 February 1798]

Coleridge organises his scene simply and progressively

towards the 'cloud-like hills and shoreless Ocean', so that his 'It seem'd like Omnipresence' is an earned conclusion. Dorothy begins systematically enough, seeing distance first, and then fetching the eye close into the foreground; but then there is a sudden jump to the 'distant prospect on the land side', and finally back out to sea and in once more to the fields. Her sea, like Coleridge's, is shoreless, but abundant and domestic, 'like a basin full to the margin'. Each element is a separate and vivid detail; we know the different greens – of orchard, wheatfield, meadow and turnip field. The scattered farmhouses, the greenness, and the 'few wreaths of blue smoke', make up a curious premonition of *Tintern Abbey*'s green – its farms 'Green to the very door', its 'wreaths of smoke / Sent up'. Dorothy's scene is full and painterly, but it is not a total composition. 'You may lament with me', she tells Lady Beaumont in 1805,

that I have not been taught to exercise the pencil. It is indeed true that I scarcely ever take a walk without lamenting it. [26 August 1805]

In detail Dorothy is always forceful; she is less happy in her statements of transcendence. 'The glittering silver line on the ridges of the Backs of the sheep' (*DWJ*, 29 April 1802) can take us further into a more splendid world than general assertions:

We lay sidelong upon the turf, and gazed on the landscape till it melted into more than natural loveliness. The sea very uniform, of a pale greyish blue, only one distant bay, bright and blue as a sky; had there been a vessel sailing up it, a perfect image of delight. [*DWJ*, 26 February 1798]

Does the wish for a ship, incidentally, come from Coleridge's imagined sea?

> With some fair bark, perhaps, whose sails light up
> The slip of smooth clear blue betwixt two Isles
> Of purple shadow!
> > (*This Lime Tree Bower*, 24–6)

We can only note, but without sharing it, Dorothy's sensitivity to the landscape's melting. A diary entry is not a poem, but so often does Dorothy make us see the details of the world afresh, that the comparison with Coleridge is instructive. Because Coleridge had an injured foot and was denied the walk with his friends, he had to conjure the landscape of *This Lime Tree Bower* out of his mind, and the effort changed his mood, and changes ours as readers, and so we see into his vision. Dorothy's plain statements are not enough. 'I never saw such a union of earth, sky and sea': this does not move us; but in her fragments and miniature scenes she arrests the essential moment that is suggestive of the merging and oneness which she found: 'The turf fading into the mountain road' (*DWJ*, 23 January 1798); 'the woodman winding along the half-marked road with his laden pony' (*DWJ*, 26 January 1798); 'The half dead sound of the near sheep-bell' (*DWJ*, 24 January 1798).

With the particular, the effects are sure: 'We drank tea at Coleridge's. A quiet shower of snow was in the air' (*DWJ*, 21 March 1798). We can savour this because the shower, the moving thing, is in fact scarcely falling: it is arrested; it is simply in the air, and quiet. Did Dorothy learn to give such a telling adjective – a *quiet* shower – to weather from the 'silent icicles quietly shining' of Coleridge's *Frost at Midnight*, from the 'silent raindrops' of Wordsworth's *Ruined Cottage* or from the 'silent weather' of his *Peter Bell*? When in Grasmere in 1802 she remarked 'a sweet sea-like sound in the trees above our heads' as she and William walked backwards and forwards in John's Grove 'for dear John's sake'[9] (*DWJ*, 23 February 1802), was she pointing forwards, or backwards to Wordsworth's early Grasmere poem where he explicitly connects as an emblem of relationship the pacing of the two separated brothers? – John

> . . . pacing to and fro' the Vessel's deck
> In some far region, . . . while o'er my head
> At every impulse of the moving breeze
> The fir-grove murmurs with a sea-like sound . . .
> ('When first I journeyed hither', 108–11)

Wordsworth uses the perception. Dorothy more often allows things to keep their separateness, and thus falls sometimes into such a happy juxtaposition that we see earth's energies and man's achievement anew. This is our sense of, for instance, her meadows of uneven ground that are 'heaving like sand – the Cottages beautiful and quiet' (*DWJ*, 22 November 1801); or her universe at once loving and mysterious when the yellow autumnal hills are '*wrapped* in sunshine, and overhung with partial mists' (*DWJ*, 10 October 1800, my italics); while at another time the universe is composed into pattern and its farthest distances brought near, when Dorothy, coming up to breathe the fresh air at Dover, looks up 'to see the stars among the Ropes of the vessel' (*DWJ*, 30 August 1802). Similarly, the creative and the humblest tasks of their life at Dove Cottage take on something of each other's quality when they find themselves side by side: William 'has been altering the poem to Mary this morning – he is now washing his feet – I wrote out poems' (*DWJ*, 13 June 1802).

Or take that favourite birch tree:

yielding to the gusty wind with all its tender twigs, the sun shone upon it and it glanced in the wind like a flying sunshiny shower – it was a tree in shape with stem and branches but it was like a Spirit of water [*DWJ*, 24 November 1801].

Dorothy de-materialises the tree, turns it into water and light – 'a flying sunshiny shower' –, and there it stays, alive, 'a Creature by its own self among' the other birch trees. As the sun went in 'it resumed its purplish appearance' and Dorothy in honesty mentions this. But there had been a moment, almost, in Wordsworth's words, of seeing 'into the life of things'. And it had been an ordinary day when Dorothy with William had come upon the birch tree, a day when her 'head had ached a little', she had 'read a little of Chaucer – prepared the goose for dinner', and then walked out. They saw the birch tree, a shower came on, and then, back home,

Sent Peggy Ashburner some goose – She sent me some honey – with a thousand thanks. 'Alas! the gratitude of men has &c.'[10] I went in to set her right about this . . .

Dorothy then had a long story about the efforts Thomas Ashburner and Peggy his wife, the Wordsworths' cottage neighbours across the way, had made to try to stop the selling of the land to a man 'fra London': 'how', said Peggy, 'they all got up at 5 o clock in the morning to spin and Thomas carded, and that they had paid off a hundred pound of the interest'; and how Peggy would 'gang out upon a hill and look owert' fields and see [the cattle and sheep] . . . it used to do me so much good you cannot think.' Dorothy clearly sympathised, as she told the hard economic story and Molly Fisher, their old servant, said cheerfully of Peggy, when Dorothy got back, ' "poor Body! she's very ill but one does not know how long she may last – Many a fair face may gang before her" '. And Dorothy and William and Mary had sat 'by the fire without work for some time then Mary read a poem of Daniell upon Learning – after tea Wm read Spenser now and then a little aloud to us. We were making his waistcoat'. And then a note came from Mrs Coleridge to say that poor Coleridge was very ill. 'William walked to John's grove' and Dorothy went out to meet him:

moonlight but it rained – I met him before I had got as far as John Batys [a neighbour's house up the road] – he had been sur-prized and terrified by a sudden rushing of winds which seemed to bring earth sky and lake together, as if the whole were going to enclose him in – he was glad he was in a high Road.

Reading Samuel Daniel (1563–1619) upon Learning would have confirmed the Wordsworths in two of their favourite tenets: first, the high worth of their poverty, which, says Daniel,

> Holds goodness in, which loose wealth would let fly;
> And fruitless riches barrener than want,
> Brings forth small worth from idle liberty
>> (*Musophilus: containing a General Defence of Learning*, 142–4)

and second, the superiority of poetry over prose. Poesy, claims Daniel, is 'The speech of heaven', and 'numbers', he says,

> wherewith heav'n and earth are mov'd
> Shew, weakness speaks in prose, but pow'r in verse.
> (ibid., 979–80)

Certainly, after reading Daniel, the Wordsworths stopped sitting by the fire without work. William got down to reading Spenser – 'now and then a little aloud', and the women worked at his waistcoat (the old 1793 vision of life in the 'humble Habitation' has become real). It was an ordinary day in November 1801, and the birch tree 'like a flying sunshiny shower' was just one thing in it – unconnected, 'a creature by its own self'. The journals always surprise like this. They have no pattern and one cannot foretell the incidents of the days recorded in them. Things are there simply because they were there.

Coherence comes not from mental structures but from feeling. Here, the separate notes of an evening at home become one through love:

– he is now reading Ben Jonson I am going to read German it is about 10 o'clock, a quiet night – The fire flutters and the watch ticks I hear nothing else save the Breathing of my Beloved and he now and then pushes his book forward and turns over a leaf. Fletcher [the carrier who often took their letters to Keswick from his peat-house across the road] is not come home. No letter from C[oleridge]. [*DWJ*, 23 March 1802]

Ten o'clock on a quiet March night four years and more since Coleridge, similarly in a mood of love, heard his cradled infant slumbering, heard his 'gentle breathings' in the 'momentary pauses of the thought', and saw the film above the fire that

> Still flutters there, the sole unquiet thing.
> Methinks, its motion in this hush of nature
> Gives it dim sympathies with me who live
> (*Frost at Midnight*, 16–18)

Even in a mood supposedly passive, in the very pauses of thought, Coleridge could not manage Wordsworth's 'wise passiveness'. He moves immediately into a sentence beginning 'Methinks', and his mind takes over. *Frost at Midnight* and its subjectivity may lie behind Dorothy's evening sounds, but her concern is William, not herself; her attentive listening to the least sound is the register of her alert love. She begins the first Grasmere Journal for William:

I shall give Wm Pleasure by it when he comes home again. [*DWJ*, 14 May 1800]

Her other reason is that keeping a diary will have a calming influence: 'I will not quarrel with myself'.

The quarrel with oneself, thought Yeats, was the very basis of poetry. For Wordsworth too, in a different way, the poet actively fosters difference and opposition: 'the poet considers man and the objects that surround him as acting and re-acting upon each other, so as to produce an infinite complexity of pain and pleasure' (Preface to *Lyrical Ballads*, 1802). Dorothy seems, rather, to seek self-forgetfulness and absorption, not dialogue. Gazing at Rydal and Grasmere in alternating moonlight and darkness, her eye moves to Grasmere Island:

when I saw this lowly Building in the waters among the Dark and lofty hills, with that bright soft light upon it, it made me more than half a poet. [*DWJ*, 18 March 1802]

The simple contrasts are effective, but Dorothy is correct in judging herself, if 'more than half a poet', certainly less than a whole one. Her reaction – 'it made me' – is helpless and passive, and never made a poet. And Dorothy knows this. Poetry is hard work, and, though the Grasmere Journals may tell us nothing critical, and it is one of their wayward charms that they do not – 'At Breakfast Wm wrote part of an ode. Mr Olliff sent the dung and Wm went to work in the garden' (*DWJ*, 27 March 1802) –, they do tell us how unremittingly hard and decidedly active the writing of poetry is. Although the Immortality Ode here is left without comment between breakfast and dung, we are made aware again and again that William is tired or 'wearied to death', or has injured himself with working.

William is the subject and the purpose of the Journals, and Dorothy has at last an occupation; as she had told Jane Pollard earlier of that first plan to live with William at Racedown, 'I shall be *doing something'*:

it is a painful idea that one's existence is of very little use which *I* really have always been obliged to feel [3 September 1795]

And were Coleridge able to be with them in the North, they would 'explore together every nook of that romantic country'; the Alfoxden intensity of looking and writing could be re-created, and 'I would once more follow at your heels', she writes to Coleridge, 'and hear your dear voices again' (*c.* 14 December 1798). Already, Dorothy is trying to re-create the past. Not surprisingly; Alfoxden was her brief university. But at Grasmere, Coleridge was a visitor only, and was troubled; Wordsworth's influence was far greater, and Dorothy records the days for her brother, to give him pleasure, and, in time, to write down possible subjects for his poems in the stories of the people she meets, stories usually of pathos and the poor.

The poor and their stories move in a realistic direction through the Journals, while running counter to these is an opposite thrust towards the ideal, and here the Garden is central. From *Paradise Lost* to Wordsworth's own poem *The Ruined Cottage* of 1797, the care of a garden is a symbol of shared love. The long lank slips of gooseberry, the broken wall and the half-choked well of Margaret's abandoned garden in *The Ruined Cottage* must have no place at Dove Cottage. One further reason for the appeal to so many people of the Journals must be that, like Dorothy, and, like her, without having to say so, we recognise the importance of these careful actions in building, with a loved person, a garden. And the love is in the detail – the getting Lockety Goldings and strawberries from the lake shore, and lemon-thyme and roots of old columbine from the hillside, the planting London Pride upon the wall, and William preparing pea sticks, and building the orchard steps. He also stuck peas (occasionally) and cleaned the well. Dorothy gathered mosses and took up orchises by the lakeside, and one evening (surely a significant planting) she 'planted a honeysuckle round the yew tree' (*DWJ*, 22 June 1800). In the fullness of the season, after the attention – 'I tied up Scarlet beans, nailed the honeysuckles &c &c' (*DWJ*, 4 August 1800) –, there is the harvest. In the August of 1800 they pulled baskets of peas, picked gooseberries, shelled peas, gathered beans. It is the deliberate recording of a dream, and its literary archetypes must include Bernardin St Pierre's novel *Paul et Virginie*, which we know from a late Journal Dorothy read in French on 7 May 1830 and which without doubt she knew in English by 1800. The novel had been published in English in 1785 as *Paul and Mary, an Indian Tale*, and then again in 1795 as *Paul and Virginia*, in a translation by Helen Maria Williams. We know that Wordsworth had admired Helen Maria Williams from his schooldays (his first published sonnet of 1787 was addressed to her), and since 'the translation of Paul and Virginia was written at Paris' – writes Helen Maria Williams in her Preface – 'amidst the horrors of Robespierre's tyranny' when 'images of desolation and despair haunted my imagination', the likelihood is that Wordsworth, with his own sad interest in France, and thus Dorothy too, knew the book very quickly.[11] The novel concerns the love of a young man and woman who are virtually brother and sister. Their story provides ruined cottages at the beginning, and an old man who traces the history of the cottages to a sympathetic listener; and in detail there are Wordsworthian parallels: the two women are abandoned mothers, the boy shows his 'sister' birds' nests, they bring plants down for the garden, they name places, and engrave inscriptions, and their emblem is the violet. When they are dead,

No marble covers the turf, no inscription records their virtues. . . . No one has since presumed to cultivate that desolated ground, or repair those fallen huts. Your goats are become wild, your orchards are destroyed, your birds are fled . . . [*Paul and Virginia*, pp. 166–8]

Both men are moved, the man who tells the story, and the man who listens; this is the framework of *The Ruined Cottage*, but the losses of the novel are total: no weeds or high spear-grass bring an image of tranquillity, as they ultimately do in Wordsworth's poem.

The drama is not so acute in the real garden and orchard, but the garden nonetheless seems to provide Dorothy with an index of feeling. She never forces a symbolism, but makes a human, perhaps a personal, connection now and then – the columbine, for instance, 'is a graceful slender creature, a female seeking retirement and growing freest and most graceful where it is most alone' (*DWJ*, 1 June 1802). But when the time is approaching for the caring for William and the garden to be shared, there is, appropriately, a heavy rain:

The Roses in the garden are fretted and battered and quite spoiled the honey suckle though in its glory is sadly teazed – The peas are beaten down – The Scarlet Beans want sticking. The garden is overrun with weeds. [*DWJ*, 5 July 1802]

The awareness that the garden will be different when Mary shares it is in the agitation of the journal entry made before Wordsworth and Dorothy leave Grasmere to go to see Mary. The swallows, whose nest has been built, has fallen down, and has been rebuilt, are there: 'they sung low . . . just like a muffled Robin . . . The moon was behind. William hurried me out in hopes that I should see her. . . . We walked backwards and forwards'. And then Dorothy moves – it is next morning – into the present tense, writing now at the moment of living, her verbs all compulsive, all 'must':

O beautiful place! – Dear Mary William – The horse is come Friday morning, so I must give over. William is eating his Broth – I must prepare to go – The Swallows I must leave them the well the garden the Roses, all. Dear creatures!! they sang last night after I was in bed – seemed to be singing to one another, just before they settled to rest for the night. Well, I must go – Farewell – [*DWJ*, 7–8 July 1802]

It is the garden that takes the pressure of feeling, just as later it signals the return to life after the first grief at the death of John – 'we turned to the melancholy garden, and put it into order' (11 June 1805). The Grasmere Journals, of their nature, are fragmentary, yet the story of the garden becomes almost a structure.

The Grasmere Journals, though finally broken off by the simple reaching the end of a notebook, have a kind of quiet last movement after that dramatic farewell to the garden. The journey to Gallow Hill, to France, back for the marriage, and back to Grasmere, is related as considered recollection; it moves at a different pace; it is a coda that builds towards its own climax – the wedding morning. This is an oblique view of a marriage. For a more conventional description of a wedding there is

Dorothy's account in 1830 of the marriage of Wordsworth's son John to Isabella Curwen; the tone, that of the fashion writer:

Five carriages conveyed the Parties to Church ... the two young Brothers of the Bride outside her Carriage kept off their hats smiling and bowing all the way. ... Fifty People sate down to Breakfast. Then departed the Bride and Bridegroom for Scotland. [5 November 1830]

At Wordsworth's wedding, the central character of the Grasmere Journals is openly Dorothy at last, not William. She formally reports her own wearing of the ring the night before and her giving it in the morning to William; this seems to be her sacramental benediction and his pledge of a continued shared life. Her tension is conveyed in the vignette: 'I saw the two men running up the walk, coming to tell us it was over' (*DWJ*, 4 October 1802). A moment of deep significance does etch on the memory the world as it happens to look at a certain instant; these two nameless men running up the walk simply and totally convey her feeling.

The Grasmere Journals end in the New Year of 1803 after gaps and despite a resolution to write regularly in future. They leave the suggestion that the marriage was a beginning as well as an ending and that the normal life at Dove Cottage continues. It was Christmas Eve:

William is now sitting by me at $\frac{1}{2}$ past 10 o'clock – I have been beside him ever since tea running the heel of a stocking, repeating some of his sonnets to him, listening to his own repeating, reading some of Milton's and the Allegro and Penseroso. It is a quiet keen frost. Mary is in the parlour below attending to the baking of cakes and Jenny Fletcher's pies. [*DWJ*, 24 December 1802]

The very last entry has a curious artistry:

Wm had a fancy for some ginger bread I put on Molly's Cloak and my Spenser and we walked towards Matthew Newtons – I went into the house – the blind Man and his Wife and Sister were sitting by the fire, ... the sister reading. [*DWJ*, 16 January 1803]

The grouping is the Dove Cottage grouping of three people, the sister reading; and somehow it suggests to us Wordsworth's own blind beggar in *The Prelude*, a blind poet-figure, with a meagre story he cannot himself read. Not surprisingly, Matthew Newton had no thick gingerbread, and though he sent some the day after, the Wordsworths bought only '2 pennyworth'. They were baking themselves. This is one of the more muted of the Journals' pathetic tales of loss and death, tales that tug against the garden and the joy of being 'Home at Grasmere'.

Death is there on the Grasmere Journals' first day: the young woman from Manchester who

had buried her husband and three children within a year and a half – All in one grave burying very dear – paupers all put in one place – 20 shillings paid for as much ground as will bury a man – a stone to be put over it or the right will be lost, 11/6 each time the ground is opened. [*DWJ*, 14 May 1800]

Two days later there is the 'half crazy old man' with his incantation – 'Matthew Jobson's lost a cow Tom Nichol has two good horses strained – Jim Jones's cow's brokken her horn.' Two more days and there is the little girl turned out of doors by her step-mother, the father not being able to stay at home, ' "She flights so" ' (*DWJ*, 18 May 1800). And Dorothy begins to use the voices of the people themselves; she is on the look-out for that 'plainer and more emphatic language' that Wordsworth in the Preface of 1800 to *Lyrical Ballads* claimed to discover in 'low and rustic life'. Dorothy records a conversation related to her by Aggy Fisher, who lived almost opposite Dove Cottage with her husband John and his sister Molly who lit fires and did cleaning and washing for the Wordsworths. Aggy had been talking with old Mary Watson. They were at Gawen Mackereth's house, where his infant daughter, Aggy's niece, was dying; Mary Watson's own son, aged twenty-three, had been drowned in Grasmere lake one fine summer

Sunday the year before. ' "We were all in trouble, and trouble opens folks' hearts" ', and so Mary, continued Aggy,

began to tell about her daughter that's married to Leonard Holmes, how now that sickness is come upon him they are breaking down and failing in the world. Debts are coming in every day and he can do nothing – and they fret and jar together. One day he came riding over to Grasmere – I wondered what was the matter and I resolved to speak to him when he came back – He was as pale as a ghost and he did not suffer the horse to gang quicker than a snail could crawl. He had come over in a trick of passion to auld Mary to tell her she might take her own again, her Daughter and the Bairns. Mary replied 'nobly (said Aggy) that she would not part man and wife but that all should come together, and she would keep them while she had anything'. Old Mary went to see them at Ambleside afterwards and he begged her pardon. Aggy observed that they would never have known this sorrow if it had pleased God to take him off suddenly. [*DWJ*, 22 June 1802]

Aggy's observation on the sick husband is sharp and unsentimental. Dorothy offers no comment. Her respect for the language and opinions of people so wholly at the mercy of God and accidents is clear in the simple telling. Years before she was to write her account of the Green family disaster, she has begun to record the obscure lives of the local people. Or, another example, there is the snatch of dialogue, evoked for Dorothy by the sight of poor old Willy's new grave by the churchyard gate. Willy Udale had had a little estate, had sunk to be an ostler at Hawkshead, had finally had to be boarded by the parish and had died a casual pauper's death. 'A boy of the house that hired him', wrote Dorothy,

was riding one morning pretty briskly beside John Fisher's – 'Hallo! has aught particular happened', said John to the Boy. 'Nay naught at aw nobbut auld Willy's dead.' He was going to order the passing bell to be told. [*DWJ*, 19 June 1802]

Again, there is Molly's sense of her good luck at being at Dove Cottage:

'Aye Mistress them 'at's Low laid would have been a proud creature could they but have [seen] where I is now fra what they thought mud be my Doom.' [*DWJ*, 5 March 1802]

By contrast, and perhaps because the account was re-collected, rather than recorded immediately, Dorothy includes only a very few of the old leech-gatherer's own words in his story, and Wordsworth in his poem 'Resolution and Independence', written a year and half later, and even further in the poem's revision, distances the man, and simplifies out the two coats, waistcoat, bundle, apron, nightcap, wife, ten children, deaths, hardship and accidents that Dorothy so carefully listed. Wordsworth takes the old man out of particular time and circumstance, while Dorothy's leech-gatherer lived and was dying in time and history. There is an appropriateness and a suggestion of an ending when at the end of her portrait she recalls his own words:

It was then 'late in the evening – when the light was just going away'. [*DWJ*, 3 October 1800]

Her recollection is written a full week after she and William met the leech-gatherer; presumably she remembered and described the encounter on 3 October 1800 as a result of a conversation with Wordsworth that afternoon:

Wm walked to Ambleside after dinner – I went with him part of the way – he talked much about the object of his Essay for the 2nd volume of L[yrical] B[allads].

So here is one of those many 'incidents of common life' (Preface to *Lyrical Ballads* 1800) offered without comment and lovingly remembered in its exactness for Wordsworth's use.

Such stories stop after the Grasmere Journals. There was perhaps no longer quite the need to collect them after the polemical Preface and the new poems in *Lyrical Ballads* had flung their challenge to literary convention. Nor was it simply that Dorothy no longer wrote a local

Grasmere Journal after mid-January 1803; she still wrote many stories. They are in the letters, but their subject-matter now is middle class: the 'impious strife' on Nab Scar at Rydal, with a hundred labourers employed 'at great wages' destroying 'trees of centuries growth' through the 'malice' and greed of neighbours, some 'topping and lopping' branches for Mr North, some felling whole trees for Lady Fleming (6 May 1809); the story of little Willy Wordsworth, aged four, and his father and mother paying an afternoon visit – 'a trading voyage', remarked Dorothy – to old Mrs Knott with the expensive *Excursion* in hand – and selling a copy, although Mrs Knott, almost deaf, had been told by others that it was above her capacity (18 February 1815); the great scene of the 1818 election at Kendal, where Dorothy, stationed at a window and determined to observe Whig strategies, thought the spectacle of Brougham's entry grand – the music, banners, horsemen and the immense multitude on foot in the driving storm – her feelings, she said, 'would have been really sublime . . . if the cause had been better' (24 March 1818); the story of the Wilberforces and their high-class servants coming to stay, nineteen of them, in Rydal, and the kitchen-maid objecting to sleeping on a mattress on the floor (18 September 1818); the story of Willy at ten years old who had too little taste for books, but 'laid out 3/6 in a *gold pin* for his shirt' (he broke it and a friend bought him another for 'ten shillings! I have now got the pin in my case' (19 January 1821)). There are many stories, sharp and entertaining. There is the same ability to catch language; but now it is in the accents of the middle class: the way 'the Luffs' place [the house of friends in Patterdale] is a paradise – 'I said to her what a delightful place – "a little pottering spot!" was her reply' (3 August 1808); or the way a friend had described a house at Watermillock that Jane Marshall was interested in as 'a perfect Rattery, a sad shattered place'

(13 April 1810). Is it that when Wordsworth ceased to need the subject-matter of the poor, Dorothy almost stopped being articulate for them? In her Scottish tour of 1822 she meets a woman with an idiot son and an ass:

By way of having something to say to the old woman, I asked if he was her son. . . . 'My own son indeed he is, as everybody knows hereabouts!'. She then began to tell us how she was wandering from house to house with a few pots . . . and had we been inclined to tarry I doubt not she would have told her whole history, and that of half the people dwelling round the Loch. [*Journals*, ii, 359][12]

Surely this is a changed attitude for one who had been 'enchanted with the Idiot Boy' (*DWJ*, 4 March 1802), and had been avid for stories and detail. One recalls Dorothy's interest in the tall beggar woman with a 'long brown cloak, and a very white cap without Bonnet – her face . . . excessively brown', and her two boys chasing a butterfly, 'wild figures',

the hat of the elder was wreathed round with yellow flowers, the younger whose hat was only a rimless crown, had stuck it round with laurel leaves. [*DWJ*, 10 June 1800]

This is a careful slow account, recollected two weeks after the encounter. And it is objective. Wordsworth in his poem on the subject makes a subjective judgment when he presents the woman as a 'weed of glorious feature' ('Beggars', 18). Dorothy is unusual in her circle in not having a refracting egotism. De Quincey, another diarist for a while, even when young, saw himself as the measure of things: 'he is a very nice boy', he said of a friend, 'about my size'.[13]

Dorothy's habit of presenting the exterior world as it genuinely appeared to her does not mean that she never focused upon herself. She sometimes presents herself with equal, and possibly embarrassing, directness. When Wordsworth sets off on a journey clearly of some importance to himself and Dorothy and probably Mary in the spring of 1802, Dorothy busies herself with putting drawers in order, picking up his scattered clothes, filing newspapers, and getting two eggs and two apple tarts for her dinner. She transplants some snowdrops, and writes at the very moment of feeling:

The Bees are busy – Wm has a rich bright day – It was hard frost in the night – the Robins are singing sweetly – Now for my walk – I *will* be busy – I *will* look well and be well when he comes back to me O the Darling! here is one of his bitten apples! I can hardly find in my heart to throw it into the fire. I must wash myself, then off – [*DWJ*, 4 March 1802]

The entry continues in the past tense for it was completed at night: 'I walked round the two Lakes crossed the stepping stones at Rydal'. Dorothy notes quite coolly now 'the sad ravages in the woods', the fir tree blown down, the reading German, the working, the reading *Lyrical Ballads*, and the writing to William. But in those first short, jumpy, present-tense sentences there is a desperateness, recognisable indeed, but rarely committed to paper. More usually, feeling is revealed obliquely. When Wordsworth's letter comes, containing presumably some more precise intimation about his marriage to Mary, Dorothy collects the letter from Yanwath – she was staying with Mrs Clarkson at Eusemere on Ullswater – but then is accompanied along the road by their good and kindly friend, the Quaker Thomas Wilkinson, and she has to carry the letter with her half-unread:

– every question was like the snapping of a little thread about my heart [*DWJ*, 12 April 1802]

When Wilkinson left she had 'time to look at the moon', and to be 'thinking over my own thoughts', and these she does not reveal. Instead, she describes two stars and the moon:

The moon travelled through the clouds tinging them yellow as she passed along, with two stars near her, one larger than the other. These stars grew or diminished as they passed from or went into the clouds – At this time William as I found next day was riding by himself between Middleham and Barnard Castle having parted from Mary.

He was riding from Mary to Dorothy – two stars perhaps? Dorothy does not comment.

When there is any speculative thought in the Journals, it is William's, not Dorothy's, and Dorothy is precise about that; the two of them are separate people: 'William lay, and I lay in the trench under the fence' (*DWJ*, 29 April 1802), not 'we lay': two subjects, two verbs. Dorothy describes the sounds (it was at about this very time that Wordsworth acknowledged how much she had always encouraged his auditory as well as his visual perceptions: 'She gave me eyes, she gave me ears', *The Sparrow's Nest*). As they lay in the trench, she heard

no one waterfall above another – it was a sound of waters in the air – the voice of the air.

Dorothy records what William thought, not what she thought:

he thought that it would be as sweet thus to lie so in the grave, to hear the *peaceful* sounds of the earth and just to know that ones dear friends were near.

Their separateness is again marked in their reactions to Coleridge's 'Verses to Sara' (later published as 'Dejection: an Ode') and to the first part of the 'Immortality Ode'. Dorothy had not commented on 27 March 1802 when she noted that 'Wm wrote part of an ode'. This 'part' was the first four stanzas, which express Wordsworth's sense that the 'celestial light' has gone, that somehow he is conscious of profound loss,

> Whither is fled the visionary gleam?
> Where is it now, the glory and the dream?

Coleridge's written response, only three weeks later, is in the 'Verses to Sara', and this is a lament upon his own grief, 'void, dark and drear'. Dorothy does comment now:

I was affected with them and was on the whole, not being well, in miserable spirits – the sunshine – the green fields and the fair sky made me sadder; even the little happy sporting lambs seemed but sorrowful to me – [*DWJ*, 21 April 1802]

The elements that help confirm her miserable spirits – the sunshine, the green fields, the fair sky and happy sporting lambs – are surely suggested by the first poem, the 'Immortality Ode'. She is seeing Wordsworth's world with Coleridge's dejected eyes; for Wordsworth himself, despite his own lack of joy, the sunshine was a glorious birth, the young lambs bounded, the birds sang a joyous song, the grief was his alone.

The next day began with a 'fine mild morning', and the now energetic Coleridge developed a plan to sow laburnum in the Easedale woods; but Dorothy,

sate under the shade of a holly Tree that grows upon a Rock – I sate there and looked down the stream I then went to the single holly behind that single Rock in the field and sate upon the grass till they came from the Waterfall. I saw them there and heard Wm flinging Stones into the River whose roaring was loud even where I was – When they returned William was repeating the poem 'I have thoughts that are fed by the Sun'. [*DWJ*, 22 April 1802]

Dorothy is still stuck with Coleridge's dejection, with the Ode's symbols of loss, its one tree and single field –

> – But there's a Tree, of many, one,
> A single Field which I have looked upon,
> Both of them speak of something that is gone –

But while Dorothy still sits by the 'single holly' and the 'single Rock', Coleridge has a plan and Wordsworth flings stones into the river and challenges his own words of loss, saying now,

> I have thoughts that are fed by the sun.
> The things which I see
> Are welcome to me

Dorothy's sympathy with sadness is linked to her interest in funerals. She gathers about her, right up through the late journals, the company of the dead, and from that first funeral in the Grasmere Journals, she is ready for death's inevitability. It was a pauper's funeral. The mourners had bread and cheese and ale, the men with their hats off. They sang a verse of a funeral psalm and then,

When we got out of the dark house the sun was shining. . . . The green fields, neighbours of the churchyard, were green as possible and with the brightness of the sunshine looked quite gay – I thought she was going to a quiet spot and I could not help weeping very much – [*DWJ*, 3 September 1800]

Wordsworth could always throw down a glove to death; the green fields and the river, certainly these, and not the individual human life, are what will abide: 'The Form remains, the Function never dies.' Yet he could attack death, and assert human achievement:

> Enough, if something from our hands have power
> To live, and act, and serve the future hour.
> (*The River Duddon*. Conclusion, 10–11)

Dorothy could only look to a quiet spot and weep very much.

Dorothy's awareness of the nearness of the dark house to the green fields, and her sympathy for the poor, made her the fitting writer of the Narrative of the Greens in 1808. The Greens, the parents of eight children, the oldest of the six still at home only eleven and the youngest a baby, had gone from Grasmere over the tops to Langdale one winter Saturday to a sale. During their walk back they lost their way in snow and storm and died on the hills. Like the Journals, Dorothy's account was written at the request of Wordsworth. Its purpose was to inform so that money could be collected for the orphaned children. She begins, rather as Wordsworth had begun *Michael*, by directing the reader to the place where 'a little stream runs over rocks and stones beside the garden wall, after tumbling down the crags'.[14] She then moves quickly through the facts to the Greens'

morsel of Land, now deeply mortgaged, [which] had been in the possession of the Family for many generations, and they were loth to part with it: consequently they had never had any assistance from the Parish . . . [p. 48]

She later returns to the connection between the morsel of land and character:

The love of their few fields and their ancient home was a salutary passion, and no doubt something of this must have spread itself to the Children . . . [p. 75]

These are the ideas of Wordsworth's 1800 poem *Michael*, in which a shepherd so identifies his own life with his land that he sends to the City the beloved son of his old age in the hope that the land can be cleared of debt and descend to the son with the same deep commitment; they are the ideas of the letter Wordsworth sent to the political leader Charles James Fox in 1801 about the sacredness of the property of the poor, and they will appear again in Wordsworth's *Guide to the Lakes*. People in the valley have close ties and they find homes for the orphans; it is Wordsworth's poem *The Brothers* in action. Dorothy addresses the Narrative 'To a Friend', and from time to time one hears echoes of the way Wordsworth's narrators addressed the reader in the early poems. 'The Cow at that time did not give a quart of milk in the day. You will wonder how they lived at all; and indeed I can scarcely tell you' (p. 49); or, 'they were never heard to murmur or complain. See them when you would, both were cheerful' (pp. 49–50). The voice of the narrator of *Simon Lee* and *The Thorn* is lurking here in Dorothy's language of conversation, and it mingles with her more moralising voice. Mrs Green had gone to a sale, but the awful event checks all disposition to harsh comments; perhaps formerly it might be said, and with truth, the Woman had been better at home. [p. 50]

Although Dorothy sees that the spirit that led Sarah Green to the sale might also have been the spirit that preserved her 'in chearful independence of mind through the many hardships and privations of extreme poverty' (p. 50), we are still not spared the notion of Sarah Green's 'bitter self-reproaches' in the 'night of her anguish' (pp. 83–4). Early and late there is a 'prosing' streak in Dorothy, and Sarah Green remains under something of a moral cloud for going to that sale. No such judgment operates when the Wordsworth family 'all went to the Sale' in 1813, and Dorothy is delighted at the

6 buff chairs, with cushions and cane Bottoms for the Study – at 9/–. . . . William bid hard for two sofas . . . We had a charming afternoon, and really it is worth while to go to a Sale, when there is so much to see from the windows. [11 September 1813]

'It would not be easy', says Dorothy in the Narrative of the Greens. 'to give you an idea of the suspense and trouble in every face before the bodies were found' (p. 51), but she does skilfully do just that, by delaying the finding – not until after a digression into the deaths of the first wife and son do we have the great shout that was uttered when the bodies were discovered. Those earlier funerals and past troubles seem one with the present trouble to the people:

how faithfully the inner histories of Families, their lesser and greater cares, their peculiar habits, and ways of life are recorded in the breasts of their Fellow-inhabitants of the Vale . . . [p. 53]

The Churchyard Book of *The Excursion* is close to this. Dorothy, well-practised, gives a fine funeral, and in her concern for truth adds a comic vignette of a local lady, Mrs North, wanting to organise everything from the subscription to the placing of the children. In her eagerness for truth, Dorothy has at least two endings; one dwelling on the pathos, pointing it by lines adapted from *The Ruined Cottage*:

> I feel
> The story linger in my heart, my memory
> Clings to this poor Woman and her Family
> (ll. 362–5)

and the other an ending with several morals, such as the finding consolation in a death that has preserved the parents from that dependence which they had dreaded and in the hope of the children's being better instructed in reading and writing. As if this double ending were not enough, Dorothy adds some notes: one on how Sarah Green's older natural daughter felt certain that she would be able to find the bodies, just as old Mary Watson knew that she would be able to find her drowned son in the lake; and one added later in pencil, on how Mary Watson was herself murdered by a younger son, a poor maniac.

The weaving of the themes of time and death and generations is more important to Dorothy than any formal sense of an ending. De Quincey in the late 1830s wrote an account of the Greens for *Tait's Magazine* and his approach offers a significant contrast; De Quincey remembers, misremembers and utterly changes Dorothy's steady treatment. While she keeps to the single cottage at the foot of Blentern Gill, De Quincey forgets the Greens for his own response to the Easedale valley: its seclusion and its 'charming combination of lawns and shrubberies', writes De Quincey, almost turning it into a park, make it a candidate for the 'happy valley' of Dr Johnson's *Rasselas*: it is, 'a chamber within a chamber, or rather a closet within a chamber – a chapel within a cathedral – a little private oratory within a chapel' (*Recollections of the Lakes and the Lake Poets*, p. 251); and four close pages of excited writing replace Dorothy's single cottage 'at the foot of Blentern Gill – . . . the only dwelling on the Western Side of the upper reaches of the Vale of Easedale, and close under the mountain'. De Quincey's response to sales is similarly lengthy and personal. He loves the social rendezvous: 'you saw old men whose heads would have been studies for Guido' (*Recollections*, p. 255). He turns Jane, aged eleven, the eldest of the children still living at home and the one who looked after the baby, into 'little Agnes' about nine years old, who later in the account is 'not much above eight'. He has her make little cakes from a little hoard of flour; he has her milk the cow and wind up the clock. He extends the period of the children's desolate heroism before they went, through deep snow, for help. The signal of distress goes through the valley like fire in an American forest; the 'towering forms of the Dalesmen' assemble – and any one of them would make the locally admired athletic Professor Wilson 'seem but middle sized' – and so it continues, the Greens themselves dwindling in the face of De Quincey's massive personal aid. Where he compels admiration, Dorothy compels belief. We seem to hear John Fleming comforting the orphan child, John Green, 'Never fear, mun! thou shalt go upon the hills after the sheep; thou *kens my* sheep!' (*George and Sarah Green*, p. 70).

Because Dorothy knows the place that she writes about in the Narrative of the Greens, the detail adds up to more than an appearance: the Greens' oaken cupboard bright with rubbing speaks of a way of life. This knowledge is absent from her accounts of more distant places. Away from home she cannot make such a meaningful selection, and there is a tendency to describe too much or too little. She saw, for instance, many different hats, caps and bonnets when she, William and Coleridge reached Hamburg in 1798, and she describes all their shapes and materials in detail. Here is her description of only one kind of bonnet:

There were Dutch women with immense straw bonnets, with flat crowns and rims in the shape of oyster shells, without trimming, or with only a plain ribband round the crown, and literally as large as a small-sized umbrella. [*Journals*, i, 20–1]

Coleridge at the same time wrote in his notebook:

Dutch women with huge umbrella hats shooting out half a yard from their eyes. [*Notebooks of Samuel Taylor Coleridge*, ed. K. Coburn, Bollingen Series 1957, I, 335]

Suddenly, the hats are alive. Dorothy's straightforward unassuming prose can for a moment seem flat next to Coleridge's buoyant language. Here is Dorothy's account of the ship voyage to Hamburg:

Before we heaved the anchor I was consigned to the cabin, which I did not quit till we were in still water at the mouth of the Elbe on Tuesday morning at 10 o'clock. [*Journals*, i, 19]

How cruelly vivid is Coleridge:

We arrived . . . after an unusually fine passage of only 48 hours – Chester was ill the Whole time – Wordsworth shockingly ill! – Miss Wordsworth worst of all – vomiting & groaning & crying the whole time! – And I . . . as well as ever I was. [*Notebooks*, I, 335]

It is Coleridge's pleasure in himself that is captivating. The journey to Goslar in 1798 was Dorothy's first trip abroad and so it is not surprising that clothes, the courses of meals, the furniture of rooms and the prices of chicken, fish, bread, tea and coffee are dominant. Dorothy is proud that the Wordsworths drove a hard bargain:

A man asked 12 marks for a pair of silk stockings, which were no better than a pair for which he only demanded 5 when he found we would not be imposed on. [*Journals*, i, 25]

This same commercial spirit in the people of Hamburg struck Mary Wollstonecraft when she was there only three years before Dorothy. Her anecdote of a duke entering into partnership with his cook in order to be

comfortably supported, leads her into a ranging specu-
lation on men and morals.[15] Characteristically, where
Dorothy gives us the exact price of something, Mary,
inexact as to cost, develops an idea.

Dorothy cultivated neither personality, nor ideas; she
kept with the visible scene, and it very often rewarded
her both in Scotland and on the Continent. Here, in
Scotland in August 1803, in a poor Highland hut, Dorothy sees a beauty rooted in common hospitality, a beauty
that is at once natural and fantastic; her mind ranges for
visual images over sky and earth, and under the earth,
and yet leans, as so often, upon the private literary
world. Her roof-beams like 'black rocks on a sunny day
cased in ice', and her fanciful underground cave with its
'colours of melted gems', seem informed both by Coleridge's *Kubla Khan*, and by Wordsworth's far-off black
rock, glistering – a knight's shield possibly, wonders
Wordsworth in his 'wilful fancy', or an entrance 'into
some magic cave / Or palace' (*The Prelude* (1805), VIII,
565–77). On the other hand, the hens indoors 'like light
clouds', the rafters' intricacy like the withered under-
boughs of a beech, and the rightness of the fading fire-
light as the family creep to their one remaining bed,
these come directly from Dorothy's observing eye:

We asked for sugar, butter, barley-bread, and milk, and with a
smile and a stare more of kindness than wonder, she replied,
'Ye'll get that', bringing each article separately. We caroused
our cups of coffee, laughing like children at the strange atmos-
phere in which we were: the smoke came in gusts, and spread
along the walls and above our heads in the chimney, where the
hens were roosting like light clouds in the sky; we laughed and
laughed again, in spite of the smarting of our eyes, yet had a
quieter pleasure in observing the beauty of the beams and
rafters gleaming between the clouds of smoke. They had been
crusted over and varnished by many winters, till, where the fire-
light fell upon them, they were as glossy as black rocks on a
sunny day cased in ice. . . . I went to bed some time before the
family. The door was shut between us, and they had a bright

fire, which I could not see; but the light it sent up among the varnished rafters and beams, which crossed each other in almost as intricate and fantastic a manner as I have seen the under-boughs of a large beech-tree withered by the depth of the shade above, produced the most beautiful effect that can be conceived. It was like what I should suppose an underground cave or temple to be, with a dripping or moist roof, and the moonlight entering in upon it by some means or other, and yet the colours were more like the colours of melted gems. I lay looking up till the light of the fire faded away, and the man and his wife and child had crept into their bed at the other end of the room. [*Journals*, i, 276–8]

Her enjoyment is plain; in an unusual confession she admits this longing for adventure:

Often have I, in looking over a map of Scotland, followed the intricate windings of one of these sea-lochs, till, pleasing myself with my own imaginations, I have felt a longing, almost painful, to travel among them by land or by water. [*Journals*, i, 289]

She liked being helped into a Highland gown and petti-coat while her own clothes dried and the young girls talked in Erse; meanwhile, the fowl was stewing in barley-broth, and the baby cried, with its old grand-mother singing 'doleful Erse songs, rocking it in its cradle the more violently the more it cried' (*Journals*, i, 281). She liked a place on Loch Lomond,

not so broad as Rydale-water, with one small island covered with trees, resembling some of the most beautiful of the holms of Windermere, and only a narrow river's breadth from the shore. This was a place where we should have liked to have lived . . . how delightful to have a little shed concealed under the branches of the fairy island! . . . I thought, what a place for Wm.! he might row himself over with twenty strokes of the oars, escaping from the business of the house . . . [*Journals*, i, 246]

There is something here of the old dream of the 'humble Habitation', but realistically adjusted to take account of the presence of children. In 1822 when Dorothy came back to Loch Lomond with Joanna Hutchinson – now in a steam boat, and not failing to voice regret for the silent oars of 1803 – she darted over the lake looking for this same islet – and could not find it (*Journals*, ii, 353). Returning from the Highlands in 1803, Dorothy and William, now without Coleridge, passed a second time through the Trossachs, and Dorothy's record of that evening walk has something of the sweetness and significance of the Grasmere Journals. This is because the place is known and has already been exhaustively (and exhaustingly) described (*Journals*, i, 271–5), and because it is loved for its personal associations. As usual, no conversation is recorded between Dorothy and William, but there is a sense of positive silence and space in the prose as we move with Dorothy along the path, so quickly various in its shade and openness, until we come to mountains, sky and light. Out of the space suddenly appear the 'two neatly dressed women, without hats', who ask their astonishing question:

I can add nothing to my former description of the Trossachs, except that we departed with our old delightful remembrances endeared, and many new ones. The path or road (for it was neither the one nor the other, but something between both) is the pleasantest I have ever travelled in my life for the same length of way; now with marks of sledges or wheels, or none at all, bare or green, as it might happen; now a little descent, now a level; sometimes a shady lane, at others an open track through green pastures; – then again it would lead us into thick coppice-woods, which often entirely shut out the lake, and again admitted it by glimpses. We have never had a more delightful walk than this evening. Ben Lomond and the three pointed-topped mountains of Loch Lomond, which we had seen from the Garrison, were very majestic under the clear sky, the lake perfectly calm, the air sweet and mild. I felt that it was much more interesting to visit a place where we have been before than it can possibly be the first time, except under peculiar circumstances. The sun had been set for some time, when, being within a quarter of a mile of the ferryman's hut, our path having led us close to the shore of the calm lake, we met two neatly dressed women, without hats, who had probably been taking their Sunday evening's walk. One of them said to us in a friendly, soft tone of voice, 'What! you are stepping westward?' I cannot describe how affecting this simple expression was in that remote place, with the western sky in front, *yet* glowing with the departed sun. [*Journals*, i, 366–7]

Wordsworth wrote a poem nearly two years later in remembrance of the scene and of their feelings. Interestingly, his poem takes off from Dorothy's ending; his concern is not the charming path, past associations and the vista of a departed sun. For him, the ground is dark, 'behind, all gloomy to behold', and, with his eye 'fix'd upon the glowing sky', he hears the woman's question. Her words are a question only in intonation; as statement they hint both at a dying in 'the light of setting suns' (in *Tintern Abbey*'s phrase) and at the energetic stepping out towards the unknown.

> The echo of the voice enwrought
> A human sweetness with the thought
> Of travelling through the world that lay
> Before me in my endless way.
> > ('What, you are stepping
> > westward?', ll. 23–6)

Where Dorothy had evoked the past, Wordsworth turns to the future.

Dorothy's account of the Continental Tour of 1820 is something of a portrait of the middle-aged British preferring to sleep in *voitures* with restless fleas than to pay six francs each for a bedroom. It is earnest as well as eager, and, again, sometimes says too much too generally and conventionally:

We were in the happiest mood for receiving the appropriate enjoyment of every pensive image or sound that met us in our progress through the dewy pastures. [*Journals*, ii, 292]

Even so, and despite Dorothy's dutiful introduction to the glacier on Mont Blanc – 'The scene is wonderfully grand and harmoniously composed' –, we are glad to have the image of Dorothy watching her party rising into and disappearing from view on the ice:

. . . sate on one of the blocks of sparkling granite with which the avalanches and torrents strew the banks. This dry seat, with the reflection of the sun from the stones put me into a comfortable glow, while I watched my Friends slowly making their way upon the stream of ice – one, and another, now on the top of a wave, now hidden on the opposite side of it. [*Journals*, ii, 285]

Dorothy would have sat for hours on a crag, the rain falling, looking at cascades on the Reuss, had people not come to stare at her. Sights still remind her of Helm Crag, Windermere and Rydal, while her bent for 'prosing' is spaciously indulged. She saw the cataract of the Reichenbach through an open window,

as in the small summer-house at Rydal. . . . It is a *tremendous* one, but wanting the accompaniments of overhanging trees and all the minor graces which surround our waterfalls – overgrowings of lichen, moss, fern, and flowers – it gives little of that feeling which may be called *pleasure*: it was astonishment, and awe – an overwhelming sense of the powers of nature for the destruction of all things, of the helplessness of man – of the weakness of his will, if prompted to make a momentary effort against such a force. What weight and speed of waters! and what a tossing of grey mist! Though at a considerable distance from the fall, when standing at the window a shower of misty rain blew upon us. To bear away a memorial of that noisy shelter, I purchased a ladle and a paper-cutter . . . [*Journals*, ii, 128]

It is good to have the ladle and the paper-cutter; conventional purchases though they are, they represent a personal choice in a journal considerably concerned with appropriate reactions in the proper places. Wordsworth's great walk of 1790 is a presence, and Dorothy quotes *Descriptive Sketches* and notes the places where 'my Brother came thirty years ago', and, with characteristic industry, when Crabb Robinson fell asleep on the Rigi, 'I', she wrote, 'took out my journal' (*Journals*, ii, 164). When it was all written up the year after, Dorothy judged it, perceptively,

so many pages – all written about the outside of things hastily viewed. [24 October 1821]

In the familiar places Dorothy's submission of eye and mind to the world she could see is her strength. It makes her letters invaluable documents: they depict the servants, children, chimneys, schools, illnesses, visits, publishing and campaigning, all the comings and goings in the life and times of the Wordsworths. And her early Journals – and the late Rydal ones in a more fragmented way – offered to Wordsworth, and still offer to us, a world noticed and a world accepted. Days begin in the morning and end at night, and whatever they bring is received. The short statements with their straightforward verbs have an innocence that does not ask us to look beyond, or to qualify, or to protest. Here is an everyday sort of entry:

Monday 20th William worked in the morning at the sheep-fold [not an actual sheep-fold, but a rhymed poem, an early version of *Michael*] – After dinner we walked to Rydale – crossed the stepping stones and while we were walking under the tall oak trees the Lloyds called out to us – They went with us on the western side of Rydale. The lights were very grand upon the woody Rydale Hills – Those behind dark and topp'd with clouds. The two lakes were divinely beautiful – Grasmere excessively solemn and the whole lake was calm and dappled with soft grey ripples. The Lloyds stayed with us till 8 o clock – We then walked to the top of the hill at Rydale – very mild and warm – about 6 glowworms shining faintly – We went up as far as the grove when we came home the fire was out – We ate our supper in the dark and went to bed immediately – William was disturbed in the night by the rain coming into his room – for it was a very rainy night – The Ash leaves lay across the Road. [*DWJ*, 20 October 1800]

The prose is unhurried, as is the life. People and place build up a calm world; the house inside seems a continuation of nature outside. The night is accepted; Wordsworth and Dorothy simply ate their supper in the dark, went to bed, and the rain, disturbing but inevitable, came into William's room. It is a domestic demonstration of 'unity entire' (Wordsworth, *Home at*

Grasmere, 151), and Dorothy has sounded this note from the Journals' beginning. The sudden juxtaposition in that early Alfoxden entry quoted above (see p. 37) makes the same assumption: 'We drank tea at Coleridge's. A quiet shower of snow was in the air . . .' We may regret that Dorothy did not record the conversation at tea, but we have, in place of so complex a particularity, a world seen as single, where even Coleridge is neither more nor less important than the presence of snow. Often, as Dorothy selects the items of her days, this more unified world seems to emerge. The walks, meetings, bakings and writings take place against a background of permanent hills and water under the colourings of the changing seasons and weather. The people in the Journals who come and go, the place-names and the domestic activities, take on a more essential tone from the setting against which they are balanced – the sky and stars, hills and water. The 'very dankish misty wettish morning[s]' and the 'beautiful still sunshiny morning[s]', the 'fine frosty evening[s]' and the 'moonlight wettish night[s]', and all the weathers, accumulate into a celebration of both change and permanence. Seasons revolve and the weather alters, but only in their constant rhythms. The passing moments that Dorothy catches, often moments of light or wind or morning mist, are still there for us to see: the birch tree 'like a flying sunshiny shower'; the reeds and bulrushes 'of a tender soft green, making a plain whose surface moved with the wind' (*DWJ*, 9 June 1800); the breezes 'brushing along the surface of the water, and growing more delicate, as it were thinner and of a *paler* colour till they died away – Others spread out like a peacock's tail' (*DWJ*, 31 January 1802); black crows flying at a distance, 'white as silver as they flew in the sunshine . . . like shapes of water passing over the green fields' (*DWJ*, 16 April 1802); shapes of mist 'passing over the sheep . . . almost [seeming] to have more of life than those quiet creatures. The unseen birds singing in the mist' (*DWJ*, 1 March 1798). In the world of the visual arts one would have to go to the sketches of Dorothy's contemporary, Constable, to find such precise arrestings of the changing moment.

Dorothy's observing eye, her outward eye, has its darker aspect. Her recording of human change and human action is also precise, but this accumulates into lament rather than celebration; for the human being, there is no renewal. Against the still mountains, people change, destroy and die, and Dorothy's writing frequently approaches elegy. Returning to Grasmere from Coleorton in 1807, she writes:

Many persons are dead, old Mr Sympson, his son the parson, young George Dawson, the finest young Man in the vale, Jenny Hodgson our washerwoman, old Jenny Dockwray and a little girl Dorothy's age who never got the better of the hooping-cough which she had when we went away. All the trees in Bain-riggs are cut down, and even worse, the giant sycamore near the parsonage house, and all the finest fir trees that overtopped the steeple tower. [19 July 1807]

Even before change has happened Dorothy sees it coming: the process is as inexorable and as hard to hold as little Peggy Simpson's chance of keeping in her hand the clean and pretty hail stones:

[she] was standing at the door catching the Hail-stones in her hand – She grows very like her Mother – When she is sixteen years old I daresay, that to her Grandmothers eye she will seem as like to what her Mother was as any rose in her garden is like the Rose that grew there years before. [*DWJ*, 13 March 1802]

Dorothy's memory was as good as her eye, or, to put it another way, as tyrannical. It enabled her to write up her recollections of the Scottish Tour (even without notes for the last part of it), but also compelled her to look for the past. 'Thoughts of last year', says Dorothy, after they have been at Dove Cottage for only one year,

'I took out my old Journal' (*DWJ*, 24 December 1801).
And in October 1802 when she writes up in her Journal
the journey back to Grasmere, now with Mary as William's wife, there is continued mingled recollection of
two previous journeys with William: the 1794 walk to
Windy Brow when they came through Staveley, 'the first
mountain village that I came to with Wm when we
first began our pilgrimage together'; and the 1799 walk
when they came to live at Dove Cottage: at Sedbergh,
'we were in the same Room where we had spent the
Evening together'. It was this 1799 journey that pro-
vided the 'dear recollections' as they pass in 1802
through Wensley:

the Bridge, the little water-spout the steep hill the Church –
They are among the most vivid of my own inner visions, for they
were the first objects that I saw after we were left to ourselves,
and had turned our whole hearts to Grasmere as a home in which
we were to rest.

She sees again 'the pathway which Wm and I took at
the close of Evening, the path leading to the Rabbit
Warren where we lost ourselves'. Why, when they were
sauntering about the graveyard at Kirby while the
horses were feeding, is the one gravestone upon which
she enlarges one erected to the memory of an unfortun-
ate woman who had been neglected by her relations?
Dorothy, cultivating her past, felt deprived of important
memories. Even her birthday contributed to her sense of
abandonment for it fell on

Christmas-day, when all persons, however widely scattered, are
in their thoughts gathered together at home . . . The Day was
always Kept by my Brothers with rejoicing in my Father's house,
but for six years (the interval between my Mother's Death and
his) I was never once at home, never was for a single moment
under my Father's Roof after her Death . . . I have been thereby
put out of the way of many recollections in common with my
Brothers . . . [to Lady Beaumont, 26 December 1805]

Those deaths and that abandonment did nothing rich

for Dorothy. She cannot use a painful past as Wordsworth could, 'thence [to] drink, as at a fountain' (*The Prelude* (1805), XI, 384–5); memory does not flow for her, a living force, into the present. The past simply stays, unchanged, its meaning, only loss. So when she is near Yanwath in 1805 with William, she tries to evoke the 'walks of my youth' when she was back at Penrith with her grandparents, walking out in the evenings with Mary and Peggy Hutchinson (died aged 24 in 1796):

The sun did not shine when we were there [i.e., in 1805], and it was mid-day; therefore if it *had* shone, the light could not have been the same; yet so vividly did I call to mind those walks, that, when I was in the wood, I almost seemed to see the same rich light of evening upon the trees which I had seen in those happy hours. At this time the path was scarcely traceable by the eye, all the ground being strewn with withered leaves ... [12 November 1805; *Journals*, i, 420]

A single line of poetry quoted in her journal in May 1802 says much, since Dorothy usually and often in these Grasmere years quotes only Wordsworth. This line she picked from an anonymous poem in the March *Monthly Review*. It has all the plangency we come to recognise in Dorothy, and, in the middle of an ordinary day, of their sowing the scarlet beans, her reading *Henry the Fifth* and finishing Derwent's frocks, and William's adding a step to the orchard steps, it casts its brief shadow:

Wept, For names, sounds paths delights and duties lost [*DWJ*, 8 May 1802]

Had she quoted the whole of the two lines, the plangency would have been greater:

> Wept, as sharp anguish came on memory's wing,
> For names, sounds, paths, delights and duties lost!

Just as Dorothy is trapped, almost imprisoned, by the appearance of things, so is she caught by the rigidity of memory. The late Rydal Mount journals, as we saw at the beginning, show the same helplessness before the passing of time. Here again, in May 1827:

beautiful green fields – cherry blossoms – all the same as 20 years ago – all but the Inhabitants [*RJ*, 5 May 1827]

Beeches & cherries very fine – John at Mrs. Luffs to dinner Willy at Mr. Pearson's – W & I quite alone this Evening as 27 years ago [*RJ*, 10 November 1827]

Twenty-seven years ago. Precisely back to 1800, the first year at Grasmere. In that early Journal, there was the building of the Garden, and the marvellous views. Here, late in life, there are sunny gleams, the day not of bright sun but gleaming, the glorious bed of anenomes, the birds. Dorothy now has only the short view and the detail, not the prospect:

I have been sticking leafy bright green twigs of Elder among my spring & winter flowers [*RJ*, 9 March 1834]

There is still the news, very fragmented, of Willy and John, Mrs Cookson and the Arnolds, Mrs Taylor, Mr Archer, dozens of people, and through all this there is the pain and the illness, and the names of the dead, one after another, and the memories: William liking to hear the rain, and Dorothy sympathetic 'in remembrance of many a moist tramp' (30 December 1834); some lines of verse that speak of 'Thoughts images of early youth'; or, on Midsummer Day 1834, a memory of the Fair held at Halifax on that day in Dorothy's childhood:

what a changed place since I used to hang out of the window by the hour . . .

In 1837 Wordsworth speaks of 'my poor Sister . . . she talks much of Halifax and her early connections there; nothing indeed seems to employ her thoughts so much' (30 December 1837). Of the rock that they called the Stone man, the rock at the top of Stone Arthur in Grasmere, Dorothy said, 'It was a sight that I could call to mind at any time it was so distinct' (*DWJ*, 24 November 1801). But having called it to mind, she could do nothing with it. Wordsworth could 'half-create' as well as perceive; he knew feelings of 'unremembered pleasure' and 'nameless unremembered acts' (*Tintern Abbey*); his consolation for the loss of the sounding cataract and the colours and forms of the mountain and the deep and gloomy wood had something to do with the power of the mind to understand itself. His wish in *Tintern Abbey* that for yet a little while he might behold in Dorothy 'what I was once' was perhaps too surely granted. Did Dorothy, with her wild eyes that noticed everything, ever move from ecstasy to Wordsworth's understanding? Or did she simply lose ecstasy? When solitude, and fear, and pain, and grief were her portion, she did indeed, at least once, in some late verses, remember Wordsworth, but she did not even then follow his exhortation – surely to understand, through the imagination as well as through memory, the mind's changing relations with the world and people. She

> thought of Nature's loveliest scenes;
> And with Memory I was there.

It was not enough. The exact eye and the precise memory inform Dorothy's writing and provide us with a universe in constant process; but, unexplored by the understanding, and finally unmodified by the aware imagination, they could not save her from the weary weight of the unintelligible world. The last existing letter (to Dora) speaks her bafflement:

They say I must write a letter and what shall it be? News – news I must seek for news. My own thoughts are a wilderness – 'not piercable by power of any star' – News then is my resting-place – news! news!

Poor Peggy Benson lies in Grasmere Church-yard beside her once beautiful Mother. Fanny Haigh is gone to a better world. My friend Mrs Rawson has ended her ninety and two years pilgrimage – and *I* have fought and fretted and striven – and am here beside the fire. The Doves behind me at the small window – the laburnum with its naked seed-pods shivers before my window and the pine-trees rock from their base – More I cannot write so farewell [March 1838]

As in her early letters, she uses literature to point her meaning, this time half-quoting Spenser, whose wood of error is itself an echo of Dante's dark wood of the middle of the journey when the straight way is lost. In Spenser's wood, significantly, the lofty trees

> heavens light did hide,
> Not perceable with the power of any starre:
> (*The Faerie Queene* I, i, 7)

For Dorothy heaven's light seems indeed hidden and the natural world remorselessly continues its activity, just as the swallows were singing to each other, and not to Dorothy, when she bade farewell to the garden. Now the activity is more violent: the laburnum shivers and the pine trees rock. Human beings have only mortality.

De Quincey as a reporter of fact and action is wonderfully unreliable, as his treatment of the Green disaster indicates; but he is skilled in the ways of his own mind and heart, and has an ability to suggest essential truths about others. His analysis of Dorothy, her reading and her writing, appeared in his essay on Wordsworth in *Tait's Magazine* (1839). His account is the most telling of all contemporary comments on Dorothy as she grew from the young woman he first met into old age. Her reading he saw as a result of her having 'obeyed the single impulses of her own heart', and, to so extensive a reader as he was himself, this seemed inevitably full of ignorances and gaps. Her manner was warm, 'even ardent', but 'checked, in obedience to the decorum of her sex and age, and her maidenly condition', and this 'self-counteraction and self-baffling of her feelings, caused her even to stammer. . . .' In her writing, she could 'produce brilliant effects', 'so bewitching an effect' from 'something or other that struck her eye, in the clouds, or in colouring, or in accidents of light and shade, of form, or combination of form.' De Quincey could hardly have known the Alfoxden and Grasmere journals; he knew some letters and had read in manuscript her account of the Scottish Tour, but he still catches the essence of her writing – 'something or other that struck her eye . . .' To call Dorothy's written words 'writings' seemed to De Quincey to be making altogether too pompous a business of it, and we understand what he means, despite our knowing more of her 'writings' than he did – we know the early journals and a whole body of letters. The self-baffling of her feelings causing her to stammer sometimes in the spoken word, and the fragmentary quality of her best 'writings', he thought might have been less of a problem had she become a regular bluestocking, had she 'condescended a little to the ordinary mode of pursuing literature.' 'It is too much to expect of any woman (or man either) that her mind should support itself in a pleasurable activity, under the drooping energies of life, by resting on the past, or on the present.' He thought that the 'little cares' of authorship would have been a minor pleasure in themselves, and that the 'more elevated cares', the 'intellectual business', would have 'done much to solace the troubles'. It seems to me that De Quincey is interestingly near the mark in his analysis but rather more beside it in his solution; Dorothy's fine eye and fine memory simply did not assemble the 'intellectual business'. The brilliant effects exist for themselves alone and cannot do otherwise. In her best 'writings' she cannot be a professional author, and she is indeed forced to come to rest on the seen past and the seen present. Yet her own bafflement notwithstanding, her writings continue to move us, so that De Quincey's final estimate seems too cool in its praise:

Miss Wordsworth would have merited a separate notice in any biographical dictionary of our times, had there even been no William Wordsworth in existence.[16]

Notes

1. Dorothy's weekday reading was only a little less earnest than that deemed suitable for the piety of Sunday. Francis Quarles (1592–1644) never quite lost his popularity as a writer of religious and ethical verse (though Charles Lamb was able to pick up 'another copy of Quarles for ninepence!!' in 1798). Dorothy may have been reading the *Emblems Divine and Moral*, with their famous wood-cuts, recently republished, 1833, or the *Divine Poems*; a copy of this last, in an early edition, 1642, is listed in the sale catalogue of books sold at Rydal Mount after Wordsworth's death. Mr Edgeworth's *Life* was the *Memoir* (1820) of Richard Lovell Edgeworth, partly written by himself, and continued after his death by his daughter, the novelist Maria. A new *Life* of Sir Christopher Wren had been published the year before, in 1833, by C. H. Bellenden Ker as one of a series of 'Lives of Eminent Persons' published by the Society for the Diffusion of Useful Knowledge. If Dorothy was not so up-to-date, she was probably reading *Memoirs of the life and works of Sir Christopher Wren* (1823) by J. Elmes. This is a handsome quarto volume dedicated to the Wordsworths' old friend Sir Humphry Davy in his role as President of the Royal Society. On the Sunday, Dorothy's reading was the Bible and most probably *Sermons* of the eighteenth-century biblical commentator, writer of tracts and mathematician, Bishop Samuel Horsley (1733–1806). An edition of *Sermons* (1827) was in the Rydal Mount library.

2. A date preceded by '*RJ*' (Rydal Journals) indicates that the quotation is taken from Dorothy's manuscript journals in the holdings of the Wordsworth Trust, the Wordsworth Library, Grasmere. The Trustees are thanked for their permission to quote.

3. A date alone following a quotation indicates that the quotation is taken from a letter and can be found in *The Letters of William and Dorothy Wordsworth*, edited by E. de Selincourt, revised by C. L. Shaver, Mary Moorman and Alan G. Hill, Oxford 1967–82.

4. A date preceded by '*DWJ*' indicates that the quotation is taken from the *Journals of Dorothy Wordsworth*, 2nd ed., edited by Mary Moorman, Oxford 1971. Quotations have been checked from the manuscript and on occasion corrected.

5. Jane had clearly recommended Robert Burns' *Poems, chiefly in the Scottish Dialect*, Kilmarnock 1786. William 'had read it and admired many of the pieces very much; and promised to get it me at the book-club, which he did' (*c.* 6 December 1787).

6. At this point in the published journal, 9 February 1798, are the first asterisks, and these indicate that in the view of the Journal's first editor, William Knight in 1897, there was in the manuscript a sentence or sentences not meriting publication: 'There is no need to record all the cases in which the sister wrote, "Today I mended William's shirts", or "William gathered sticks" '. Unfortunately the manuscript has not been seen since Knight made his transcript and so the puzzling weeks with Coleridge and the omissions remain. However, one is inclined to believe that Dorothy wrote no more, or very little more, than is printed of the Alfoxden Journal between 20 January 1798, when it begins, and 9 February, when the first asterisks occur: a comparison with the Grasmere Journals – for which manuscripts do exist – shows that Professor Knight was reasonably conscientious in indicating omissions. There are no further asterisks until 28 February, when possibly a whole day's entry was omitted. 14 March has also gone and four days in April, 19 and 21–23. Knight seems to have decided on partial omissions for 3, 10, 16 April and 9 May. The greater frequency of Knight's asterisks towards the end of the Journal is in keeping with what appears to be its natural development: what began as a book of descriptive exercises was turning into a record of daily events.

7. *The Memoirs of the Author of the Vindication of the Rights of Women* (1798), written and compiled by her husband, William Godwin.

8. *DWJ* 20, 22, 26 January, 15 February, 24 March, 1798.

9. John's Grove. Now, mainly a beech wood; then, a fir grove, above Dove Cottage, past How Top Farm, on the old road to Rydal. Wordsworth had discovered a path in it worn by their younger sailor brother John during the first months of 1800. John left to become captain of the East Indiaman the *Earl of Abergavenny*. He was drowned in 1805 when his ship struck rocks off Portland.

10.   Alas! the gratitude of men
                     Has oftner left me mourning
    – the concluding lines of *Simon Lee, the Old Huntsman*.

Another example of Dorothy's application of Wordsworth's poetry to her everyday life.

11. Since this was written a copy of the novel in Williams' translation, in an edition of the mid-1790s and containing Wordsworth's signature, has come to light; it is in private hands.

12. '*Journals*' following a quotation indicates that the quotation is taken from *The Journals of Dorothy Wordsworth*, ed. E. de Selincourt, Macmillan 1952.

13. From a letter from De Quincey to his sister Mary, 12 March 1799, from *Thomas De Quincey: An English Opium-Eater, 1785–1859*, Robert Woof, Dove Cottage 1985, p. 33.

14. Quotations here are taken from Dorothy Wordsworth, *George and Sarah Green: A Narrative*, ed. E. de Selincourt, Oxford 1936.

15. Mary Wollstonecraft, *Letters written during a Short Residence in Sweden, Norway and Denmark* (1796), ed. Carol H. Poston, University of Nebraska 1976, pp. 188–90.

16. This and the foregoing quotations from De Quincey's essay are taken from *Recollections of the Lakes and the Lake Poets*, ed. David Wright, Penguin 1970, pp. 131–2, 202–6.